WIRED

Being Connected to the Life of God Within You

Dionne van Zyl

Forward by GRAHAM COOKE

WIRED

Being Connected to the Life of God Within You

DIONNE VAN ZYL

THE FOUR ELEVEN FOUNDATION, INC.

WHAT OTHERS ARE SAYING ABOUT THIS BOOK

It will change your lens

"Wired" is a book that will affect the way you view life in Jesus by empowering you to develop the same lens about yourself as the Father has for the Son. That lens will create a mindset which will revolutionize your thinking and will set you free to engage with God at all levels of life.

Graham Cooke
Author and speaker
Brilliantperspectives.com

An amazing work

I have read countless Christian books; this may be the last one I will ever need to read. Wired is not another book about Grace, it is a book about life. It is about the life that is promised in the scriptures but is seldom seen. Abundant life. Jesus' life. In Wired, Dionne brilliantly tackles the core issues of identity and purpose. He expresses the wonder of the cross. He fearlessly tackles the difficult questions. But more importantly, he unveils the Holy Spirit in a unique and beautiful way that demystifies His person and His purpose. This book is not theoretical, it is real life, and every assertion is founded in scripture. I am so grateful that he chose to share his wisdom and experience in the pages of this amazing work. You must read Wired!

Wayne Lowery
Captain, Delta Airlines

Refreshing

It is a wonderful and fresh view for those who are seeking more understanding of who we are in Christ Jesus and who He is in those of us, that have received Him as Savior and Lord, and how we are "Wired" for success in life, through the Grace of God.

William Fisher, MTh.
Pastor, Northlands Church

First Printing, 2016,
10 9 8 7 6 5 4 3 2 1

Published by:
The Four Eleven Foundation, Inc.
PMB 331, 2566 Shallowford Rd, Ste 104, Atlanta, GA 30345

Published in the United States of America

Title: Wired
Subtitle: Being connected to the fountain of life within you.
Author: Dr. Dionne van Zyl
ISBN 978-0-9859-6351-4

This book is dedicated to my wife, Bridget.

She is my best friend, co-heir in Christ, and my business partner. She lives many of the truths in this book that I have only recently come to understand.

"He gave you a human spirit to give you the capacity to know Him."

Wired 2
Dionne Van Zyl 9
Graham Cooke 11
Introduction 15
The Fountain Of Life 20
God's Spectacular Creation 31
Understanding The Heart 44
The Flesh 56
God's Feelings About Feelings 65
Your Eternal Nature 75
Your Will Be Done 82
Enjoying A Clear Conscience 95
What Really Happened At The Cross? 106
Your Identity In Christ 117
You Are Truly Forgiven 127
Your Gift Of Righteousness 139
Your New Nature 147
You Are One With Christ 154
Revolution Of Goodness 162
God Is Restoring Life In You 172
Why Jesus Is Praying For You 180
Walking In Grace 185
Meet My Friend, Holy Spirit 197
Free Your Mind 209
Living A Worry Free Life 220
Good Thoughts Release Life 228
The Functions Of The Human Spirit 238
The Supernatural Ability To Receive 249
The Supernatural Ability To Relate 259
The Supernatural Ability To Respond 268
Practical Next Steps 279

ABOUT THE AUTHOR

DIONNE VAN ZYL

Dionne van Zyl is a minister of the gospel, a businessman, an author, and a family man.

He was ordained as a minister in 1987. He has served in the local church as an elder and pastor of local churches in Atlanta and his native city of Pretoria, South Africa.

His adult life has focused on family, ministry, and business. He became an American citizen in 2002 and lives in Atlanta, Georgia with his wife Bridget and his son, Luke. His three adult children are happily married, serving the Lord in the same local church, and successfully pursuing their careers.

He has led several companies as CEO in technology, financial services, real estate, and private equity.

His engineering degree helped him launch his first software business. He also has a BA Theology degree, an MBA and Ph.D. in management. Dr. Van Zyl translated his thesis into a business book that co-lated the best management practices from around the world into a single system called Acuity (acuitybook.com).

Today, he leads a portfolio of businesses while pursing ministry as the Chairman of The Four Eleven Foundation - a non-profit organization that is focused on equipping leaders and pastors for the work of the ministry. The foundation launched its first website in 1996 which was one of the first Christian websites on the Internet.

FOREWORD

GRAHAM COOKE

"Wired" is a book that will affect the way you view life in Jesus by empowering you to develop the same lens about yourself as the Father has for the Son.

That lens will create a mindset which will revolutionize your thinking and will set you free to engage with God at all levels of life. Enabling you to overcome every obstacle, both within and around your real life circumstances is a major part of this book.

Finally, it will provide you with a whole new vocabulary that will seriously upgrade your normal daily conversations and will radically affect both your prayer and worship language.

I like the way "Wired" is laid out. Like a stairway, each step takes you up from the mundane to the majestic. It has landing places to stop and ponder what you are seeing and learning.

"Wired" has five major elements of revelation covering every segment of the book. These are:

1 - 8 How we are made in God's image.
9 - 14 The Cross and the new man.
15 - 19 Walking in the Holy Spirit.
20 - 22 Upgrading your thinking.
23 - 27 What supernatural means and signifies.

This book exposes you to God's long-term purpose for His people. You will find that wrong norms, poor mindsets and an incorrect frame of God will give way to a sense of wonder about who He is for you!

"Wired" enables you to understand how you are made new in Christ. It pulls you into a place of encounter where you will never again allow the physical world to pull you out of your inner world of the spirit.

Learning how to free the mind is a crucial part of this excellent work. Especially demolishing strongholds by taking thoughts captive. Just knowing the difference between worldly and Kingdom thinking is huge. I particularly enjoyed the 'think test.'

The segments on the Holy Spirit are remarkable as are the sections on functions of the human spirit and how to respond to the supernatural requirements of being made in the image of Jesus.

Whether reading this book yourself or studying it with a groupof friends, "Wired" will make you think. It will create dialogue. It will empower your hunger and desire for more.

It is a book that raises your sights and provides you with a more powerful expectation that the God of love is deliberately and passionately going to engage with your story and journey.

Dionne is a dear friend. He is profoundly intentional, a deep thinker and a passionate worshipper.

Our conversations together have been present/future in scope, practical and pragmatic regarding the outcomes of life and how to get there, and above all full of wisdom, love and laughter.

What Jesus has done for Dionne you are about to experience!

Graham Cooke
Author and speaker
Brilliantperspectives.com

ACKNOWLEDGEMENTS

Thank you to my dear wife, Bridget, for her endless encouragement and being my primary sounding board.

I'd like to honor the late Rev. David Griffiths who was my spiritual father, mentor and the man who taught me the scriptures and cultivated a deep love for the Lord.

Thank you to my son, Ross who helped me conceive the inner man model presented in this book.

Thank you to my son, Bruce for managing the production, printing and promotion of this book.

I deeply appreciate the feedback and help from all my children, Lindsay van Zyl, Liesl and Jackson Webber, Jordan van Zyl, and Luke van Zyl.

Thank you to the test group who gave me such helpful feedback specifically, Greg and Michelle Haswell, Daniel Cline, Wayne and Carla Lowery, William Fisher, Michael Tapajna, Robin Johnson, Terry and Dot Mitchell, and Kim van der Riet.

INTRODUCTION

It was exhilarating and frightening at the same time. I had never been rock climbing before. I was in good hands though. My friend, Kim, was a talented rock climber and he knew exactly what he was doing. His parents had met in the mountain club and he had spent many years climbing and even saving his dad's life on the rocks - catching him when he slipped and fell. His dad was knocked unconscious and was hanging upside down with a broken collar bone. Kim managed the entire situation on his own.

I had great confidence in Kim's ability. I looked up at the steep rocks ahead of me following the rope upwards knowing that he was up there belaying me. He was securely perched on a ledge with the rope in his hands. It was terrifying looking down at the tops of the trees way below me while I had a tiny rock edge on which to secure my footing in addition to my finger tips trying to hold on. I worked my way up slowly looking for the next slither of rock on which to commit my weight. The more progress I made the more frightening it became.

Being a slender college student, I had the advantage of a good power to weight ratio. My greatest advantage was my age - I still believed I was invincible. Ignorance is bliss at times like these. As I painstakingly worked my way to the top, I kept myself from looking down. I looked up and followed Kim's instructions and his encouragement. When I finally reached the summit, I felt elation. The view was spectacular. The reward was worth the effort.

In many ways, this illustrates my previous view of the Christian life. I saw it as a tough and seemingly impossible climb. God's standards are so high and so demanding and I was afraid of what it would demand from me. The more I progressed in God the further I could fall. It seemed like the stakes kept getting higher and the climb more difficult the longer I did it.

I hoped Jesus had the rope firmly in His hands and that there was enough grace to catch me if I slipped.

I had no idea that Jesus climbed this rock face so that I did not have to! What a shock it was to discover He has fully qualified me because He knew I could never do it on my own.

I aspired to the impossible idea that my performance would only be rewarded if I acted flawlessly and persevered to the top. I believed that my performance determined my standing before God. I wanted to enjoy His love but I felt disqualified and unworthy. It was all so confusing.

In 2007, something extraordinary happened to me. I had a crisis of faith. I realized that there was little difference between my life and that of my non Christian neighbors. I discovered after 30 years of being a Christian, there was not much that differentiated me other than a Christian world view. My life was not one I would have described as full of power and abundance. I did not feel that I was fully accepted in Christ. When Jesus talked about giving us life in abundance, I could not relate. Somehow, a powerless life had become normative.

I do not know how it happened but suddenly powerlessness was no longer acceptable. I wanted to truly know Him and enjoy His presence. I could not be satisfied with a type of Christianity that was more philosophy than enjoying the life Jesus promised.

I came to see that many, like me, were trapped in this type of intellectualized Christianity. I made a mental assent to the truths of the gospel but did not live in their reality. I had moments when I felt the love of God but did not live there permanently.

My wife, Bridget, and I made a radical decision. That decision would transform our lives in a way we never imagined. **This book is a presentation of that transformation.**

We decided to become people of faith. We wanted what Jesus talked about when He promised us abundant life. We wanted to live in His love and acceptance permanently and not just visit it occasionally. We wanted to enjoy the inheritance that the apostle Paul called glorious. We wanted to see our lives transformed by His power. We longed to see the lives of others redeemed and rescued by the power of the gospel.

We made the decision to radically serve God. That crisis changed the trajectory of our lives and took us down a very different path.

I am pleased to say that we are ecstatic about the outcome. Our lives are much more satisfying and fruitful than before. God is so good and so kind!

We realized that we had the wrong mindset and framework about the gospel and the kingdom of God. God had already placed us on the top of the mountain and asked us to dwell with Him there. What a shocking difference it has made!

This book is the presentation of that mindset change. I will share the breakthrough understanding of how God has wired us to enjoy Him and the how to walk in the Spirit that leads to a fulfilling and powerful life.

I hope you enjoy the truths and the revelation that changed our lives forever!

CHAPTER ONE

THE FOUNTAIN OF LIFE

The Bible tells us of a wonderfully romantic story about a young woman who is working on the family farm. She works in the field every day alongside her brothers who are very tough on her and treat her harshly. In her culture, women who worked outside and who were exposed to the sun, were considered less beautiful than those who did not. In the story, she asks herself, "How can anyone love me because of the way I look?" Shortly thereafter, she meets a very handsome man in the fields and it seems that it's love at first sight. They fall madly in love and meet often. She's so amazed that she has found love and, even more, amazed that this incredible guy would love her.

One day she's out in the field working when she hears the King's processional party approaching. She sees the resplendent outfits of all the officers and a magnificent carriage. Like all the workers in the fields, she goes down on one knee out of respect for the King. To her horror, the King's carriage stops in front of her. He steps out and walks towards her. She looks at his feet and his beautiful shoes but out of respect she does not look up. She hears her name being called and she looks up into the face of her lover! She's utterly stunned! All this time, her lover was the king and she did not know it. She is speechless as he takes her hand and brings her to her feet. He leads her into his carriage and takes her back to the palace.

It is like a fairytale and no doubt she feels it is surreal. She, a simple field worker, now a princess in the palace. She is assigned attendants who bathe her, clothe her, and teach her the behavior of a Queen. She has to learn to step into her new role, learn to command with authority, and be a lover to the most powerful man in the Kingdom. She must trade her farm worker mindset for a royal mindset.

She often meets with the King in their special garden as they spend time together as lovers. Afterwards, she notices that she carries His fragrance with her. She's absolutely captivated by His love and he is captivated by her. An entire book of the Bible known as Song of Songs is dedicated to this one story.

What does the story mean?

The story tells of God's love for us. We are born into sin and the poverty of that lifestyle. He seeks us out and comes to rescue us. He loves us while we are still laboring intensively in the field of self-effort. Jesus came to die for us and rescue us from the field of sin and put us in our rightful place at His side in the palace. As fantastic as the story is, the reality in the spiritual realm is even more wonderful for you and for me. Jesus, our heavenly bridegroom, came to Earth to rescue us and to make us His own. It was never His intention to leave us in the field.

How some tell the story

Now imagine that we tell the story differently. Suppose that the carriage stops in front of the young woman, the King steps towards her while her head is bowed and says, "All your debts are forgiven." He steps into the carriage and rides off. It is amazing how many believers live as though that's the story! Jesus came to forgive us our sins — that is true and wonderful. But far more importantly, Jesus came to rescue us — redeem us — from the life we had and to place us in a place of spiritual authority so now we are seated with him in heavenly places, as the Scripture says. He did more than forgive our sins, in fact, He broke the power of sin and death over us, redeemed us from the life we once knew and made all things new. The Scripture says that anyone who comes to Jesus becomes a new creation and all the old things passed away and everything becomes new. This means that your old nature of sin died with Christ and now you are resurrected in newness of life with him. You have been given a new nature! You are a brand-new creature! You are the object of His love!

You are a fountain

In the story, the King tells His bride, "You are a garden fountain, a well of flowing water streaming down from Lebanon" — Song of Songs 4:15.

This whole story is an Old Testament picture of a New Testament reality You are the object of Jesus' love. You are His dearly beloved. You are not an orphan but His dearly beloved who captivates Him. This radical idea — that we are the object of God's love — is the key to living an abundant life — a bit of Heaven on Earth.

It is more important for you to know how much God loves you than how much you love God. The first goal of every believer is to become a good receiver. We need to receive His forgiveness, receive the new nature that He gives us, receive His fellowship, and receive His love. If you want to grow up in your faith and become a strong believer, then become a strong receiver.

When we learn to receive from the Lord, His love overflows in our hearts into every aspect of our lives as we will explore in great detail later in the book.

This overflow is essential to living the abundant life. Jesus was not offering us a great life or a wonderful life or a sufficient life. He was offering an abundant life. Look at this verse in Romans 5:17, "For if, by the trespass of the one man, death reigned through that one man, how much more will those who **receive God's abundant provision of grace** and of the gift of righteousness reign in life through the one man, Jesus Christ!".

It is fascinating to study the word "abundant" in this verse. The bottom line is that it means superabundant in quality and quantity.

The picture of a fountain

Think of a fountain with multiple layers and the water that's flowing in it is flowing so abundantly that each level is overflowing to the next level which is overflowing to the level below that — like the drawing below.

As you sample the water you discover that it is the clearest, most stunning quality of water that you've ever tasted. This is what Jesus was offering us! He offered us the quality of life that was meant to overflow in our lives to others around us. When others taste the quality of the life that flows through us they are drawn to the Father.

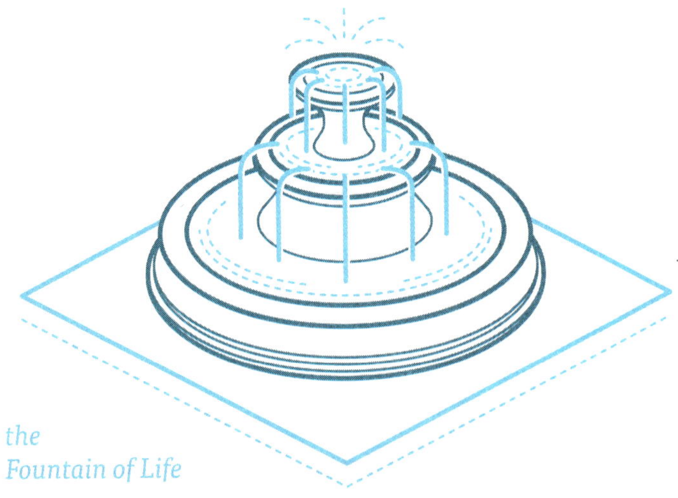

Why abundance is so important

This idea that the Kingdom of God is received and not achieved is core to understanding abundant life. If we believe that our performance earns us God's favor, we are misled and we spend our days trying to earn what we already have. We are favored because of Jesus.

This is the great exchange that took place at the cross: everything there that was due to you was put on Jesus; and everything there was due to Jesus was put on you. Think about this for a moment. All your sin, shame, curses, hopelessness, poverty, low self-worth, purposelessness, and meaninglessness was all put on Jesus at the cross. And all that was due to Jesus - the Father's favor, the Father's love, forgiveness, purpose and meaning, joy, peace, abundance, hope — was put on you! Wow! That is the gospel of Jesus Christ! It is good news!

Great receivers are people that receive so much that God's love overflows into every aspect of their lives and then that overflows to everyone around them. These are people who live the abundant life.

Unfortunately, externalized religion has robbed us of this precious truth. It has taught us a performance-based system in which we have to earn everything in God. Nothing could be further from the truth. Everything we have, we have received from God by grace and grace alone.

External versus Internal life

What I mean by externalized religion is that the external events of our lives drive all our primary decisions including how we feel internally. If things are going well externally, we feel life is good. Likewise, when we are facing challenges and difficulties, there is internal toil and pain.

The Lord is teaching us to live an internal life filled with His love and power. The Lord is teaching us how to live inside out. Allow me to explain: when we come into relationship with Jesus an eternal life force is ignited within us. This power flows from our inner being into the outer world. It is His abundant life flowing through us that transforms us internally and transforms our external world. This is the mechanism by which Heaven invades Earth. It is an extraordinary life filled with Heaven's power, the Father's love, and the exceptional inheritance that Jesus purchased on the cross.

Jesus paid an extraordinary price so that we could live extraordinary lives. This does not mean that we will live lives without difficulties, challenges or even deep loss. It means that we live life differently — with purpose and power.

Jesus said that the Kingdom of God is within you. But most believers live lives of an externalized religion. We picture God somewhere in Heaven when we pray. We're asking an external God to fix our external world so that we can feel better internally. This is not how the Kingdom of God works. When Jesus said that the Kingdom of God is within you, He was being quite literal.

When you became a believer — born again — your whole inner world was transformed and made alive to God. The Father, Son, and Holy Spirit came and made their home in you. Now you carry Heaven's primary occupants inside you. You have become part of His eternal domain in which you are in Him and He is in you. He exists outside of time and space and the Bible says that even the Heaven cannot contain Him (I Kings 8:27). You have now entered His realm and you host His divine presence.

How many of us picture God within us when we pray? How many of us realize that Heaven's solution has been provided in Jesus within us. You were called to an internalized relationship with God and not to an externalized religion.

The extraordinary benefits of an internalized relationship

There is a different way to live. There are so many promises in the Scriptures that are beautiful and enormous in scope — but many of us find them hard to believe. We either think that these spectacular promises are not for today or we believe that they may be true for others but not for us.

In a very deep way, we disqualify ourselves from all that Jesus purchased for us on the cross. Externalized religion constantly tells you that you do not qualify! Externalized religion is based on personal performance and is a works-based gospel. But, the gospel of Jesus Christ is based on grace and invites you to an internal relationship with Him based on His perfect performance on your behalf! You are now fully qualified because He has qualified you!

Even the basic construct that "God is good" is difficult for many believers to truly believe. When life makes no sense and they find themselves suffering for no apparent reason, it is difficult to believe that "God is good", and more precisely, that God is good to them personally.

The truth is that God means for us to live victoriously through difficult times and He means for us to enjoy the extraordinary benefits of living an internalized relationship with Him - even when life makes no sense.

The love of God is the purest and most attractive commodity in the universe. One taste of that love and you are addicted forever! We were designed by God to be addicted to Him. We were designed to have His love overflow in our hearts.

The love drain

It is sad that so many believers have a hole in their hearts. Any love that He shows them is immediately absorbed and they seem to remain dry. The world is filled with people with a love deficiency. The hole in the heart has a way of seeking love to fill it and it will do anything to attain that love. Some may seek it in physical things like drugs or illicit sex. Others may seek it in intellectual ways. There are those who will seek to validate their value in the pursuit of success. The bottom line is: every single human being, regardless of race, ethnicity, sex, education, intelligence, wealth, or geographic location, deeply desires to be loved. We were designed to be receivers of His divine love. There is no end to the supply of that divine love — it flows freely and in abundance!

The love fountain

We were born thirsty, but we were designed to be satisfied. In John 7:37-38 Jesus makes this astonishing claim, "... Jesus stood and said in a loud voice, "Let anyone who is thirsty come to me and drink. Whoever believes in me, as Scripture has said, rivers of living water will flow from within them."

It is interesting that Jesus did not say, "river" but rather "rivers". This again speaks to the idea of abundance. When we come to Jesus and we believe in Him, His love flows in us and quenches the thirst within us. The mechanism is that we come to Jesus and drink and drink and drink and drink. Perhaps it has been so long since you have enjoyed His love and now it is time for you to learn to become a drinker — of the right sort!

The Scripture goes on to tell us in the very next verse what Jesus meant by this. Look at verse 39, "By this, he meant the Spirit, whom those who believed in him were later to receive. Up to that time, the Spirit had not been given, since Jesus had not yet been glorified." The Holy

Spirit is a person of the Godhead who delivers the Father's love to us in superabundance and in exceptional quality. We will spend a good portion of the book discovering who this glorious Holy Spirit Person is. He is not a force, a topic or someone to be feared. He is God - a member of the Godhead. When we learn to "walk in step with the Spirit" as the Scripture says, rivers of living water flow through us and saturate our entire beings and once saturated, overflow to everyone around us.

The destructive power of droughts

From 1958 to 1961 China saw one of the worst droughts ever recorded in human history in which it is estimated that between 20 and 40 million people died. What makes this even worse is that just 50 years earlier, in 1907, China's drought killed more than 24 million people in just a few months. That is about the same amount of people that died in World War II - 60 million. One country within a 60-year time frame suffered such catastrophic disasters brought about by the destructive power of droughts.

The world's megadrought

An article in USA Today, MEGADROUGHTS - A THREAT TO CIVILIZATION stated, "Megadroughts are what Cornell University scientist Toby Ault calls the "Great white sharks of climate: powerful, dangerous and hard to detect before it's too late They have happened in the past, and they are still out there, lurking in what is possible for the future, even without climate change." Ault goes so far as to call megadroughts "a threat to civilization." Megadroughts are defined more by their duration than their severity. They are extreme dry spells that can last for a decade or longer, according to research meteorologist Martin Hoerling of the National Oceanic and Atmospheric Administration."

The greatest megadrought of all is for God's love. This drought has lasted for centuries. The law of the Old Testament has been used as a means to judge people. Sometimes the church has used this standard to judge pre-Christians and each other.

The primary reason for this is not that church people are bad, but rather that they themselves are experiencing a love-drought. When we as believers are overflowing with the love of God in our own lives, we cannot help but overflow to everyone around us. In the same way that water flows naturally, God's love will flow through us effortlessly and relentlessly. It does not require a performance mindset to "love others". That is why Galatians 5 speaks about the fruit of the Spirit as love, joy, peace, patience, kindness, etc. As my daughter Lindsay so eloquently puts it, "The fruit of the Spirit is not a holy to do list but rather a natural reflex of the Holy Spirit in us."

This is how they will know that we love God

Jesus said in John 13:35, "By this everyone will know that you are my disciples if you love one another." The way people are brought to Jesus is through love. It is kindness to others that shows the kindness of God. Judgment and condemnation do not bring people to Christ. The Scripture says it is the kindness of the Lord that leads people to repentance (Romans 2:4).

If we are truly serious about changing the world for God, we must become serious about receiving His love for ourselves. This is not a one-time event. Learning to be a great receiver is a lifetime process. Every day we learn to receive more and more of His love until we naturally overflow.

In the upcoming chapters, we are going to get to the detail of how this works. In this next chapter, we are going to explore how God has wired us — how the inner man works.

2

CHAPTER TWO

GOD'S SPECTACULAR CREATION

When God created the universe, He made it to be overwhelmingly spectacular and extravagant. You only need to walk out on a beautiful clear evening and stare up at the sky and think about the stunning nature of creation. Everything about creation speaks about God's all surpassing creativity in diversity, color and unimaginable size!

Living on a pinhead

A few years ago a friend of mine was teaching his science class about the size of the solar system. He used a 15-inch beach ball as the sun. He explained to his class that they would scale the solar system according to the beach ball. This would make the Earth about the size of a large pinhead and Jupiter would be the size of a ping-pong ball. He had one child hold the "sun" on the one side of a field and then he had different children each holding a planet the scaled distance from the sun. It surprised the students that the pinhead Earth was one-third of a football field away from the beach ball and Jupiter was more than two football fields away. This would put Pluto 1 mile away! He asked them how far it would be to the next beach ball (sun).

It turns out the next beach ball would be in Shanghai, China given that this beach ball is in Atlanta, Georgia (6,800 miles away).

If you're traveling at the speed of light to the next sun (Proxima Centauri) it would take 4.3 years to get there. Let your mind absorb the idea that there are about 100 billion stars (beachballs) in our Milky Way galaxy. That is just one galaxy and it is such an enormous thing that we cannot visualize it. Now imagine 100 billion galaxies that make up the universe! Scientists now believe that the visual part of the universe (the hundred billion galaxies) is only 4% of what the universe is made of. They're estimating that another 21% is made up of dark matter and the remaining 75% is made up of dark energy. They call it dark not because of its color but because they have no idea what it is.

Now here is the real piece of stunning information: of all the things in God's creation, mankind is God's finest — made in His own image!

The human spirit

That same incredibly powerful Creator made you. The way He made you is equally as spectacular and wonderful. He gave you a core — a human spirit that empowers you to do things that reflect His very nature! He designed you to be amazing and to reflect the wonder of His own creativity and brilliance. He built that into your human spirit — that eternal part of you that is not bound by space and time.

It is the human spirit that causes us to look for something greater than ourselves to worship. It gives us the instinct that there is much more to life than the physical universe.

He gave you a human spirit to enable you to have the capacity to know Him. This is truly mind blowing! This capacity dramatically exceeds that of the human mind. Because of your spirit, you have the ability to interact with the spiritual universe and have an intimate relationship with the Creator himself!

The human spirit does indeed have extraordinary power. When you came to Christ your spirit was made alive to God. What kind of power should that release? The Bible refers to the human spirit as "the spirit of a man" and in some cases calls it the "inner man." Obviously the term "man" is referring to a person and used in the sense of mankind. Scripture clearly teaches that men and women are equal in value, equal in inheritance and coheirs in Christ. (Any references in this book to "man" is using it in the biblical sense and obviously includes both men and women equally.)

The human spirit is the core and eternal part of every human being. When you understand that your human spirit is the most powerful part of your being, you can discover what life is like when you live from your human spirit in fellowship with God Himself.

Your human spirit has such other-worldly capabilities. It can have fellowship with an eternal and timeless being who created you - God himself! Think about it for a minute. An enormously powerful, perfectly loving Being who lives outside of time and space — that dwells in a realm the human mind does not understand — lives in you!

If you have encountered God as your Lord and Savior, it is your human spirit that informs you that He is real and your experience of His love is deeply satisfying and substantial. Your mind may have a difficult time trying to explain this to someone else. You just know that you know. And even when your emotions cannot confirm His love for you, it is your spirit that informs you that He is ever present and will never leave you or forsake you.

Past, present and future are simply limitations of the human experience.

When you have fellowship with an infinite and eternal Being, these limitations are of no consequence. Your human spirit has the ability to reach above limited human capabilities and fellowship with the very Being that created you. Is that not awesome?

God meant for us to live a life that derived its power from a realm beyond human limitations — beyond the physical universe. Jesus came so that we may have this kind of life! It is time for us to discover the life-giving power of this realm which the Bible speaks about in simple terms. Our human spirit is the primary means by which God delivers His life-giving power.

Perhaps you know the feeling when you understand something in your inner being and then sometime later your mind begin to understand it. Your human spirit has the capacity to receive revelation from God long before your mind can understand it. Revelation is a gift from God that is received. God loves us to understand and know His love. To more fully understand how this works, let's take a look at how God put us together — our biblical anatomy.

You are wired by God

Like your physical body, your inner man is made up of different parts Down through church history, church leaders have provided various models to help people understand these parts and how they work together Having studied many of these different models, I think it is more useful if we go back to Scripture and see how it explains how God wired us. It is important to understand that the Bible does not provide a clear break up of these inner world parts.

The classical model

The classical model says that we have a body, soul and spirit. In this model, the soul is defined as having three parts: mind, will, and emotion. This is a fairly popular model that has some serious problems with it. The main problem is that there are only two scriptures that are used to support this idea. What we're looking for are the broad strokes of Scripture that show consistency throughout the Old and the New Testament.

Furthermore, the classical model does not have a good explanation for the word "heart" or a clear understanding of how "conscience" fits in. My biggest concern with the classical model is that it leads to misconceptions of our life in Christ. It infers that our spirit is saved and it is up to us to fix the rest of our inner world — the mind, will and emotions. Scripture, however, paints a far more wonderful picture of our inner man.

Building a model from key biblical words

The Bible uses words such as soul, heart, spirit and body. Scriptures like Proverbs 2:10 say, "For wisdom will enter your heart, and knowledge will be pleasant to your soul"; or Isaiah 26:9 which says, "My soul yearns for you in the night; in the morning my spirit longs for you. When your judgments come upon the Earth, the people of the world learn righteousness." These verses use the terms heart, soul, and spirit. There are many Scriptures that use these terms and often in the same verse.

So what does this mean? The Bible is providing us an insight into how our inner world works — the biblical anatomy of the inner man.

I have been researching this topic for over 30 years. As part of that process, I reviewed many of the early church fathers and their teachings. It is insufficient to use a Greek or Hebrew lexicon to determine the scope of these words and their biblical meanings because the meanings overlap one another as we will discover. In my research I came across a very helpful book called *The Ways of Our God: An Approach to Biblical Theology* by Charles H. Scobie. The book references many other theological sources and theological works that relate to the subject we are discussing here. (I am not promoting Scobie's book in its entirety but the very helpful research summary he provides in Chapter 16.) He provides an excellent summary of some of the great theological works on this subject.

A key to understanding our inner world: sets and subsets

A breakthrough in my thinking came when I realized that the Scriptures do not present the parts (that make up our inner world)as separate pieces, but rather as parts of each other. The best way to explain this is to think of some basic math you used at school. Please don't switch off because I use the term "math". I am referring to the idea of sets and subsets. Let's use as an example the idea of people as a set and then add males as a subset of people:

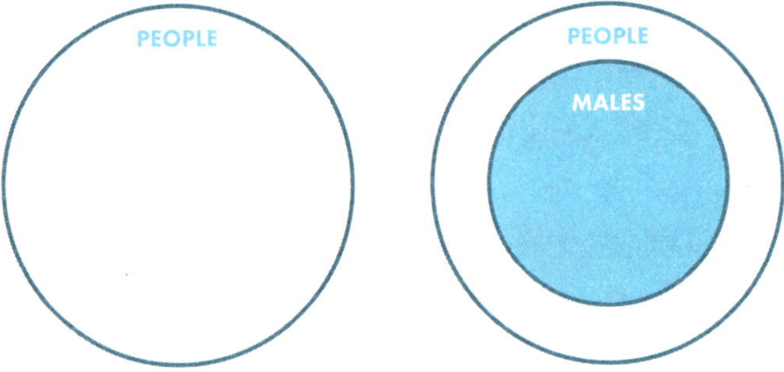

Taking it to the next level we can further add another subgroup under males called boys. Clearly boys are a subgroup of males, like this:

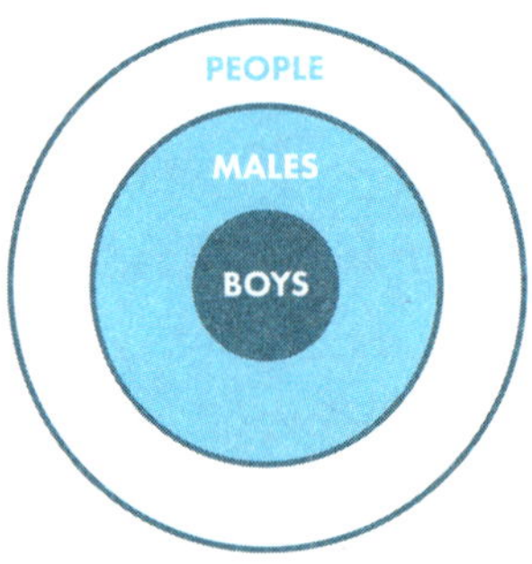

I know this is very basic, but I want to make a simple point that will help us as we explore the biblical model that Scripture presents. This simple idea of sets and subsets is very important. The key idea here is that when we speak of people, we automatically include males and because we include males we automatically include boys. So, in our simple example, boys are people too (a big surprise, I know). The big idea here is to get that boys, males and people are not separate entities We cannot say that they are three species of beings: people, males, and boys — although many women have wondered about that! We clearly understand that there is only one species called people and that includes the subgroups. In the same way, when we speak of *males*, we are automatically including boys.

Here is what I want you to learn from this example: Any set you refer to automatically includes the subsets under it. The bigger group includes all the sub-groups under it.

The biblical anatomy of the inner man

Let's see how Scripture uses this idea to explain the components and subcomponents of our inner man. What is fascinating is that these concepts are consistent in both the Old Testament (Hebrew) and the New Testament (Greek). So it will be helpful for us to take a short review of these words to understand what the Bible means by them.

The soul

In both the New Testament and the Old Testament, the word that summarizes our entire inner being is the word soul — it is the biggest group (set). In the Old Testament, the Hebrew word for soul is "nephesh" and in the New Testament the Greek word for soul is "psyche".

Both of these words refer to our **sense of self.** It is the *"I"* or the *"me"*. It refers to our own **sense of identity** of who we are. The Oxford Dictionary says, “We associate psyche with things of the mind, but to the Greek spsukhē meant ‘breath, life, soul,’ which then developed into the idea of ‘self’. This base is involved in the first element of the science terms psychology.” So the Bible teaches that you have a soul — your inner life — your sense of self — **the “I” — your true self.**

Charles Scobie says, “Psyche can mean one’s life (Mark 10:45; John 10:11; Phil 2:30), and in some texts is virtually the equivalent of the self: “What shall it profit a man, if he shall gain the whole world, and lose his own soul?” Mark 8:36 (KJV) can be rendered “What does a man gain by winning the whole world at the cost of his **true self**?”

The heart

At the center of your soul is your heart. We get this from the Old Testament Hebrew word “Lab” which is translated as *heart* in English. This is the same translation used in the New Testament for the Greek word “kardia.” The *heart* is at the center of the *soul* and consists of your mind, your will, your emotions and your conscience. We will spend time later in the book exploring the details of the *heart*. Throughout the Bible we see enormous evidence that God is all about the *heart*. Now we understand that the *soul* includes the *heart* at its center as shown in our diagram. Remember from our previous discussion about sets and subsets, that the *heart* is not separate from the *soul* but part of it. So if we talk about the *soul* we automatically include the *heart*.

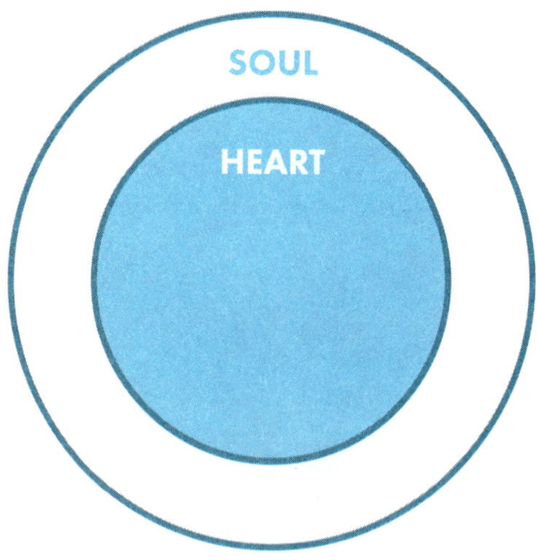

Charles Scobie adds, "The term kardia, ... refers to the center and source of the whole inner life, with its thinking (2 Cor 4:6) and volition (Rom 2:15) as well as emotions, wishes, and desires (1:24). Jesus emphasizes the heart as the center of human motivation: "Out of the heart come evil intentions..." (Matt 15:19; cf. 5:28). But those who respond to God's grace can become "pure in heart" (5:8). The heart can be "hard and impenitent" (Rom 2:5), but it is also with the heart that one believes (10:10), and God's love can be poured into our hearts through the Holy Spirit (5:5)."

The spirit

The next word we want to explore is the Hebrew word "ruwach" which is translated as *spirit* in English. The Greek equivalent in the New Testament is the word "pneuma." This word literally means your life force, wind, or life energy. This is the eternal part of the human being that has a direct relationship with our eternal Creator. It is the part of us that goes beyond human capabilities and provides us access to the abundant life Jesus promised. Now we can complete our diagram. At the center of the *soul* is the *heart*. At the center of the *heart* is the *spirit*.

Charles Scobie writes, “The term pneuma, usually translated *spirit*, can also mean wind (John 3:8) and breath (2 Thess 2:8)…. Pneuma denotes the life or vital force, what gives life to the body, so that “the body without the spirit is dead” (Jas 2:26). To yield up the spirit means to die (Matt 27:50), … It is that aspect of a person which is most open to the divine Spirit (Matt 5:3; Rom 8:16)”.

This is why we are considered to be dead in our sins and when we came to Jesus we were made alive to God.

Once again, when the Bible talks about the soul it is automatically including the heart and the spirit. Likewise, when it talks about the heart it is automatically including the human spirit. This will clarify much of how Scripture uses these terms interchangeably. Now we can understand that our spirit is part of our soul - at its very center, in fact. If we talk about the heart we know that it is part of our *soul* and at the core of the *heart* is the *spirit*. If you understood that last sentence, you got it!

The fountain analogy

Let's go back to our fountain diagram. Perhaps you can imagine that you are standing on a balcony overlooking a plaza that has a fountain in it. As you look down on the fountain, you see the wide bowl at the bottom (the *soul*), a smaller bowl on top of that (the *heart*), and spouting water out the center, you see the fountain (the *spirit*).

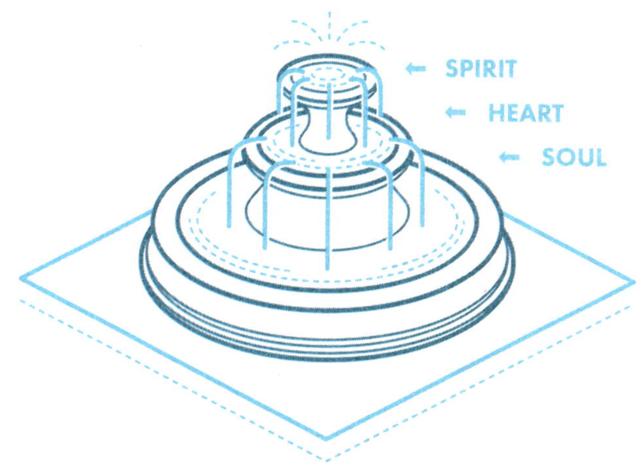

When we come to Christ, our *spirit* is made alive to God. His life in us is the source that overflows through the rest of our inner being. He is our life, energy, and power. Notice that God's life overflows into our *hearts* and from the overflow of the *heart*, His life flows into our *soul*.

What does this mean? It means that God's life that flows from our *spirit* overflows to affect our entire being. It washes our mind, will, emotions, and our conscience - our *hearts*. The overflow of the heart determines who I think I am. It **defines** me as the Bible says in Proverbs 23:7, "For as a man thinks in himself (nephesh — soul), so is he." Jesus intends to change your entire identity of who you think you are. He means to transform your sense of self into His own image. He came to give you new life and life in abundance It requires abundance of life in your *spirit* to overflow into your *heart* and that abundance to further overflow into your sense of who you are — your *soul*.

The new life you now have in Jesus is powered by the life resident and flowing in your spirit. That is why Jesus said in John 7:37-38, ".... Let anyone who is thirsty come to me and drink. Whoever believes in me, as Scripture has said, rivers of living water will flow from within them."

The great solution to the world's megadrought

We have now found the secret to the world's spiritual Megadrought. The promise of the Holy Spirit to satisfy our dry and parched souls is God's plan to bring life to a desperate world — starting with you and me.

CHAPTER THREE

UNDERSTANDING THE HEART

One of the great heroes of the Bible is a man named David. He grew up in Bethlehem and his job as a young boy was to watch the sheep. This occurred during the reign of Israel's first King named Saul. This was an interesting time for Israel since they decided that they'd rather have a king than be ruled directly by God himself. They told the Lord that they wanted a king just like every other nation and God gave them Saul.

One day God told the prophet Samuel to go to the house of Jesse to name a successor to Saul. Samuel did as the Lord instructed and Jesse brought all his sons before the great prophet. A critical thing happened during the selection process. The Lord told Samuel not to look at the outward appearance but to select the person of the Lord's choosing — the one who had the right heart. When Samuel stood before the oldest son, God told him, "Do not look on his appearance or on the height of his stature, because I have rejected him. For the Lord sees not as man sees: man looks on the outward appearance, but the Lord looks on the heart."

Interestingly, David was not at this meeting but was out in the field tending the sheep because he was the youngest.

Back to the story. When each of the sons of Jesse had stood before the prophet and none were selected, Samuel asked if Jesse had any other sons David was brought in from the field and anointed King.

From that point on, David's life is a story of extremes. On the one hand, David killed a bear and a lion with his bare hands while protecting the sheep, which gave him the confidence to take on Goliath - the greatest of the Philistine soldiers. On the other hand, David committed some of the most serious sins recorded in the Bible, like adultery with Bathsheba and arranging the murder of her husband. He was the father of Solomon - one of the greatest kings recorded in the Scriptures, but he was also the father of Absalom who led a rebellion and caused great bloodshed.

David was a man of great military conquest. He gathered mighty men around him — each of whom was a greatly respected general in his own right. Yet God chose this man to record the personal struggles and victories of his own heart. Many of the Psalms were written by David and we have a wonderful journal of David's inner struggles. We see his longings for God and his unyielding trust in his heavenly father.

David lived in almost constant warfare — which in some ways reflected the constant war of his own heart. He loved God desperately and God gave him one of the greatest compliments given to any man when He said, "David is a man after my own heart". (Acts 13:22: God testified concerning him: 'I have found David son of Jesse, a man after my own heart; he will do everything I want him to do'.)

Despite David's failings, the cry of his heart was, "Create in me a pure heart, O God, and renew a steadfast spirit within me" (Psalm 51:10). Notice how David refers to his own heart and the center of his heart — his spirit.

Is it a good idea to follow your heart?

The prophet Jeremiah said, "The heart is deceitful above all things and desperately sick; who can understand it? I the Lord search the heart and test the mind, to give every man according to his ways, according to the fruit of his deeds" (Jeremiah 17:9-10).

If the prophet Jeremiah is correct, this seems like very bad advice indeed! Why would we follow something that is deceitful and sick? Jesus confirmed the idea that the heart is the source of our problems when He said, "But the things that come out of a person's mouth come from the heart, and these defile them. For out of the heart come evil thoughts--murder, adultery, sexual immorality, theft, false testimony, slander" (Matthew 15:18-19 NIV.)

Before you become too depressed, let me share some really good news with you. Jesus came to cure the sick heart. He came to give us a new heart. He said, "Let not your hearts [kardia] be troubled. Believe in God; believe also in me" (John 14:1). "I will give you a **new heart and put a new spirit** in you; I will remove from you your heart of stone and give you a heart of flesh" (Ezekiel 36:26 NIV). Here we see that when God gives us a new heart, He must also give us a new spirit since the spirit is at the center of the heart and is a part of it.

Our hearts are made new when we invite Jesus to take residence. At no point are our hearts made pure by our own good deeds. It takes an otherworldly miracle to transform our hearts and make them fit to receive Jesus. Christ comes to dwell in our hearts through faith (Ephesians 3:17). When we believe that God sent Jesus to die for our sin and raised Christ from the dead, we initiate the greatest miracle of all: we are translated from the Kingdom of darkness into the Kingdom of light. We are transformed from sinners to saints. We are given the gift of righteousness and our hearts are made new and pure by divine miracle. "May he strengthen your hearts so that you will be blameless and holy in the presence of our God and Father when our Lord Jesus comes with all his holy ones" (1 Thessalonians 3:13 NIV).

This mind-boggling miracle culminates with the Father, the Son and the Holy Spirit taking residence in us. Jesus said, "On that day you will realize that I am in my Father, and you are in me, and I am in you" (John 14:20 NIV).

The whole process is then sealed with a guarantee: "set his seal of ownership on us, and put his Spirit in our hearts as a deposit, guaranteeing what is to come" (2 Corinthians 1:22 NIV).

Back to our question: is it a good idea to follow your heart? If you're following the heart that has been renewed and now inhabited by God himself, it is an excellent idea to follow your heart. However, if you are living a life in which your heart is still informed by the flesh, it is truly a bad idea.

The components of the heart

Now that we've come to understand that the heart is at the center of our soul — at the core of our inner being — we've learned that the heart is made new when we come to Christ and accept His finished work on the cross.

We've also discovered that the heart consists of four components:

- mind
- will
- emotions
- conscience

Perhaps a simple diagram of the heart may help us understand this better:

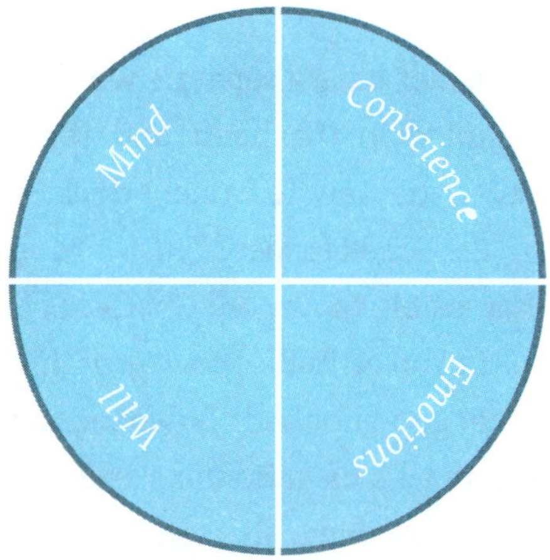

Remember, that the heart is the middle circle of our model. So let's add back the soul and spirit to see what the new picture looks like. This picture looks a bit like a wagon wheel doesn't it? That's a pretty good analogy in helping us understand that the soul connects us to the world, and at the hub of our soul is our human spirit — which connects us to the spiritual realm. It's all held together by the heart.

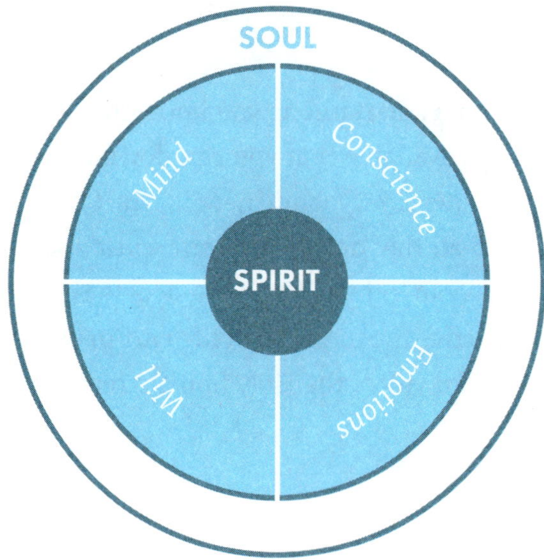

Now we will take a closer look at each of the heart components.

The mind

The Old Testament does not have a separate word for "mind." It seems that the mind is included in the heart and there is no distinction between them. However, the New Testament does have a separate word for mind.This word in the Greek is *nous*. This word refers to our intellect and the part of us that is able to reason. Charles Scobie points out that this word can also refer to an attitude or a way of thinking as in Romans 12:2. The mind is neither good nor bad. It depends on what is feeding it. That is why the Scripture tells us in Romans 1:28 that we need to renew our minds so that we may be able to discern God's will.

It may be helpful to think of the mind as an instrument — a bit like a computer that responds to inputs. Just like a computer, it can be programmed. The Bible calls this programming "renewing the mind." This is what Paul is talking about in Romans 12:2, "Do not conform to the pattern of this world, but be transformed by the renewing of your mind [nous]. Then you will be able to test and approve what God's will is--his good, pleasing and perfect will."

Spiritual apps

If you have a tablet or a smart phone you know that there are hundreds of thousands of apps available that you can download and use on your device. The marvelous thing about new life in Christ is that He has already downloaded all the "apps" into your spirit and encourages you to activate them in your mind. When we access the what Christ has freely given us, we active the fountain of life within us. In the same way that some apps stream video, the Holy Spirit streams His love and life into our hearts.

Look at this fascinating verse in 1 Corinthians 2:9-12, "However, as it is written: 'What no eye has seen, what no ear has heard, and what no human mind has conceived'-- the things God has prepared for those who love him — these are the things God **has revealed** to us by his

Spirit. The Spirit searches all things, even the deep things of God. For who knows a person's thoughts except their own spirit within them? In the same way, no one knows the thoughts of God except the Spirit of God. What we **have received** is not the spirit of the world, but the Spirit who is from God, so that we may understand what God has freely given us."

This is indeed a fascinating Scripture because it says that God has gone before us and prepared wonderful things — so wonderful that no mind can conceive them naturally. It takes a supernatural revelation for us to understand what God has for us. Paul goes on to say that the Holy Spirit searches these deep things in God and reveals it to our human spirit. Our human spirit then informs our minds! Isn't this wonderful? It shows that we can, and in fact, should understand what God has freely given us. I love the fact that Paul says God "has revealed" these things to us by His Spirit. It's a past tense event. The day you were saved, everything God had prepared for you was downloaded into your human spirit which your mind can access. This process of accessing revelation is how our minds are renewed.

Later on, in verse 16 in the same chapter Paul says, "For, who has known the mind of the Lord so as to instruct him? But we have the mind of Christ."

So the key question here is, how can we have the mind of Christ and yet still need to renew our minds? Our model shows that the answer is in fact very simple and straightforward. The mind of Christ is fully available to you in your spirit — you have it and can fully access Christ's thoughts! When you do this, your mind becomes renewed and you begin to think like Him in every way. The more you access these thoughts the more your mind becomes programmed to think like Jesus.

Paul goes on to say that when we allow our minds to be programmed by the world, we develop worldly thinking.

John confirms this idea in 1 John 2:20 and 27 when He says, "But you have an anointing from the Holy One, and all of **you know the truth.** .... As for you, the anointing you received from him remains in you, and you do not need anyone to teach you. But as **his anointing teaches you about all things** and as that anointing is real, not counterfeit--just as it has taught you, remain in him."

Speaking of the mind, this blows mine! The key thought here is that John is saying the Holy Spirit is the anointing we receive in our human spirit and this anointing teaches us about all things. This confirms what Jesus stated when He said that the Holy Spirit would come and lead us into all truth. Now this does not mean that we do not have to listen to any sermons or go to church. The Holy Spirit uses leaders and pastors to teach us and help us access truth.

Have you ever sat in a sermon in which the preacher was clumsy in his presentation, but somehow something deep in your heart told you that what he was saying was indeed the truth? Your spirit has the ability to inform you what is true and what is not true. The opposite is also true. You can listen to a non-christian professor who presents an eloquent speech but something deep inside warns you that this is not the truth. That is why we can listen to the views of the world and know that it is not of God. Your mind can be impressed by worldly thinking but your spirit knows it's wrong. Likewise, you can listen to a clumsy message and be put off in your mind (or emotions) but your spirit confirms that it is the truth.

It is great when we can hear truth presented that is both eloquent and life giving, but we cannot dismiss truth simply because it does not com packaged in a way we prefer it.

God has built a powerful function into your human spirit in which you can know truth. The Holy Spirit is our kind and gentle teacher who leads us into all truth. That is why Jesus said the Kingdom of God is within you. So, whether a preacher is eloquent or clumsy, the truth can still be conveyed and bring life change. It matters little that the presentation is exciting, emotional or intellectually stimulating. It only matters that what is being preached contains life. Something deep inside of you is stirred when the truth is presented. It does not matter if that is a sermon, a casual conversation or something you're reading in the Scripture. That internal witness from your inner being is the Holy Spirit confirming to you the truth of what you're hearing.

Later in the book we are going to discuss the functions of the human spirit.

The deep thoughts of God

Another word that is translated mind in the New Testament is the Greek word "dianoia". This word is interesting because it adds another dimension to how thinking works as a believer. The word can really be broken up into two parts: dia (through) and noia (thoughts), i.e through thoughts or deep thoughts. The inference here is that the deep thoughts of God flow from our spirit into our mind. These "through thoughts" flow through our spirit and into our minds.

Paul talks about this in Ephesians 4:17 when he says, "This I say, therefore, and testify in the Lord, that you should no longer walk as the rest of the Gentiles walk, in the futility of their mind [nous], having their understanding [dianoia] darkened, being alienated from the life of God, because of the ignorance that is in them, because of the blindness of their heart [kardia].....and be renewed in the spirit [pneuma] of your mind [nous]."

Here Paul is unpacking for us the mechanism we have been discussing. He is telling us that we should not walk as those who do not know the Lord. Their thinking is futile because their "deep thoughts" mechanism does not work. That is why they are alienated from the life of God that would be in their spirit. But since they are not believers they have no life to access. As a result, their hearts are blind and they cannot see.

You are not like that. Your spirit has been made alive to God and, therefore, your "through thoughts" mechanism is working correctly and enlightens your thinking. These thoughts from God create understanding and cause your heart to see. This is how we hear God's voice.

Paul goes on to say that if you are a believer who is living like an unbeliever there is a solution for you: be renewed in the spirit of your mind — access the spirit-mind connection. Paul is encouraging you to allow the deep thoughts of God to flow from your spirit into your mind and this will cause your heart to see all that He has for you. These wonderful things that God has prepared beforehand for you to walk in can only be understood through spiritual revelation and not through intellectual pursuit.

It gets even better. God gives us these deep thoughts so that we can know Him. The apostle John confirms this idea when he says, "We know also that the Son of God has come and <u>has given us understanding [dianoia],</u> **so that we may know him who is true**" (1 John 5:20 NIV).

John is making it clear that *dianoia* - God's deep thoughts — are given to us by Jesus so that we can know Him and access eternal life.

The more you allow God's thoughts to flow into your mind, the more powerful your mind becomes. My spiritual father, David Griffiths, believed that when we live by the Spirit, our IQ goes up. These thoughts include wisdom, understanding, creativity, innovation, and thoughts that produce life in others. What an incredible capability that God has so freely given us. Perhaps you have not been aware of this magnificent capability that God has built into the core of your being. Now you can see and understand why the Scriptures say you should not be worldly in your thinking — futile in your thinking. As believers, we do not look to the world to shape our thinking because, by its very nature, it is futile at its core. Our thinking is informed and shaped by the eternal Creator Himself. What kind of life would you live if, from today on, you accessed His thoughts and your mind was being continually renewed to think like Jesus?

For us to live such powerful and exceptional lives, Jesus had to set us free from sin and from worldliness. Externalized religion will simply command you to stay away from worldliness without showing you that you have access to eternal life in your inner being. Once again we see that the Kingdom is received and not earned. How wonderful the grace of God is.

CHAPTER FOUR

THE FLESH

Some people say to me, "This sounds too fantastic and aspirational. What about the flesh?" It's a fair question and we need to address it. To do so we need to understand what the Bible means when it uses the term *flesh*. Just like in the previous chapters, we want to avoid our own traditions in this matter and take an open-minded look at what the Scripture says for itself on the subject.

The biblical words for flesh

The Hebrew word "basar" means body or *flesh* and was never used in a sense of evil. The references of the Old Testament refer to flesh in a good sense or at least in a neutral sense.

The real problem for the use of the word *flesh* is found in the New Testament, especially when the word "sarx" is used. This word generally means the physical body, but Paul added a unique use of the word. Paul sometimes used it in its neutral sense referring to the human body, but when it became a gateway for sin, Paul used the word "sarx" in a negative way. It is really important to understand that Jesus himself had a "sarx"— a human body which of course was not evil.

Charles Scobie writes, "Jesus himself, in Gethsemane, warned Peter to watch and pray, for "the spirit indeed is willing, but the flesh is weak" (Matt 26:41//Mark 14:38); here flesh is not evil, but it does provide a point of entry for temptation. In John's Gospel Jesus contrasts what is born of the flesh and what is born of the Spirit (326), and says that while the Spirit gives life, "the flesh is useless". Any idea, however, that the flesh in and of itself is evil or the source of evil is negated by the strong emphasis in the Johannine literature on the fact that Jesus himself "became flesh" (John 1:14; 1 John 4:2; 2 John 7; cf. also Heb 2:14; 5:7)."

Paul is not saying that we have two natures one spiritual and one flesh. He is not confused by the fact that all things were made new when we came to Christ as he says in 2 Corinthians 5:17, "*Therefore if anyone is in Christ, he is a new creature*; the old things passed away; behold, new things have come!" He is clear about the fact that when we come to Christ our old man is crucified with Him and we are raised in newness of life just as He was raised. We will discuss this in a later chapter and show that when you come to Christ you are given a new nature.

Paul is telling us not to allow the physical world to invade our inner world. He does not want us to become worldly in our thinking and allow our physical bodies to become a gateway for sin. He says in Philippians 4:7, "Then you will experience God's peace, which exceeds anything we can understand. His peace will guard your hearts and minds as you live in Christ Jesus."

Perhaps you have been subjected to poor teaching that says your spirit is made holy and your flesh is sinful. That is simply not what Scripture teaches. In fact, the Bible goes on to say that your body is the temple of the Holy Spirit. This is God's **Holy** Spirit and He cannot inhabit an unholy place as His temple. This means that part of your salvation included your **body** being made a holy temple to be inhabited by the Holy Spirit.

Evil does not exist in physical matter

Evil does not exist in physical matter nor does it exist in your physical body. Charles Scobie explains further, "Paul lists 'the works of the flesh' in Gal 5: 19-21, but he does not imply that sin has its root in the flesh. Nor does his list consist of what a modern reader might understand by "the sins of the flesh"; although the list includes sexual sins, two-thirds of the terms do not refer to this but denote various forms of breakdown of human behavior, e.g., enmity, strife, jealousy, anger, etc."

What war are we fighting?

Paul makes it clear that we are fighting a war. He says, "For though we walk in the flesh, we do not war according to the flesh" (2 Corinthians 10:3). This means that we live in a human body (in the flesh) but we do live by the standards of worldliness and therefore, our battle is not against other people (flesh and blood) but against the powers of darkness and the kind of thinking the enemy is sowing into the world.

That's why he says that the weapons we use are not worldly but come from God and can tear down arguments that stand up against godly thinking, "We demolish arguments and every pretension that sets itself up against the knowledge of God, and we take captive every thought to make it obedient to Christ" (2 Corinthians 10:5 NIV).

Paul is saying that you have power weapons that can stop your mind from being programmed by worldly thinking and force these worldly thoughts to submit to the mind of Christ within you.

The deep thoughts of God that are coming from your spirit are way more powerful than the futile thoughts coming from the world. God has placed in your hands weapons that can take worldly thoughts captive and make them obedient to Christ. You are extremely well-equipped to be the one who influences the world with God's thoughts rather than a victim who is subject to worldliness and futile thinking.

Jesus has made you powerful for a reason. He wants the Kingdom of God that is within you to be released to this world. That is why the Scripture says that it is the kindness of God that leads people to repentance. God wants to show His love to the world through you. He wants to demonstrate the power of that love to a broken world. For you to be effective, you need powerful weapons. These weapons can destroy sinful and worldly thinking that keep people in bondage.

A practical example

Philippians 4:7 says, "And the peace of God, which transcends all understanding, will guard your hearts and your minds in Christ Jesus." Here we can see that it is God's peace that comes into your heart and it passes all understanding. Notice what is happening here: God's peace is placed in your spirit and that peace cannot be naturally understood. In fact, it passes all understanding. When your heart needs guarding, it's the peace of God that you need. When you feel vulnerable and anxious, God's peace comes into your spirit and it flows into your heart. You feel emotionally more settled and calm even though you cannot understand how it works or why it works. This releases you to make better decisions — decisions not based on fear but on peace.

It gets even better. Colossians 3:15 says, "Let the peace of Christ rule in your hearts..." So where does the peace come from? It is from Christ What is your role? To let it rule! It is not your job to create peace or generate a feeling of peace, but to *let* Christ's peace reign in your heart. Your job is to simply authorize God's peace in your life — to allow it — to give it permission to reign in your life. Notice the Scripture does not say we should grow in peacefulness. It does not encourage us to manufacture or imitate peace, but, in fact, the Scripture wishes us to have the real deal — the peace of Christ himself. God wants you to live an extraordinary life and that means letting Christ's peace not only *reside* in your heart but ***rule*** in your heart. When peace rules, Christ rules.

Anxiety is based on fear — fear of potential events in the future. We take these fearful thoughts captive by reminding ourselves that the Lord is our fortress, our protector, and our help in times of trouble. If you are facing fearful events in your life right now, take a moment. Close your eyes and become aware of the presence of the Lord and let His peace flood your heart. Now, let that peace take a permanent position and reign. When Christ's peace reigns in your heart — your heart is guarded against fear.

You can choose to allow fear to rule or Christ's peace to rule. It is so simple a child can do it. The Bible says the weapons of your warfare are powerful and that fear must submit itself to Christ's peace — it has no choice whatsoever.

Your mind may struggle with the concept but your spirit knows it is true But is it really that simple? We can simply "let" the peace of Christ rule in our hearts? The answer is: absolutely yes! When you came to Christ you were given a new authority which came with being one with Christ. Think of it this way: before two people get married they each have their own possessions. When they get married, they share everything. In much the same way, you were married to Christ and now, get to share all His stuff — including His peace. It's yours — you simply have to *let* it rule in your heart.

Remember the deposit that was made in your spirit when you came to Christ? Everything you need for life and godliness has been given to you. 2 Peter 1:3 says exactly that. "His divine power has given us <u>everything we need</u> for a godly life through our knowledge of him who called us by his own glory and goodness." Paul confirms what Peter says in 1 Corinthians 3:20 - 23 when he reminds us that all things are ours in Christ Jesus.

The Scripture is full of such commands. The New Testament gives many of these commands that tell us to put off the old nature, put on the new man, be hospitable, be patient, be kind, be generous, etc. There are 1,050 such commands in the New Testament. How can the Bible simply tell us to put off and *be* this and *be* that? The answer is so simple it may astonish you.

All the things that Scripture commands you to *be* **have already been given to you.** Everything you need for life and for godliness has been freely given to you in Christ. When the Bible instructs you to do something it's because at the core of your being it exists in you. This is the reason the Scripture says things like "be bold" or "be patient." These things are yours and you are being encouraged to walk in your new nature — to draw from Christ who lives within you. It is wonderful that we do not have to imitate these attributes. The Scripture is not asking us to manufacture these things but to walk in them. When we come to realize that we have a powerful spirit inhabited by the creator of the universe, we find we have access to everything that we need.

Intellectualized Christianity is a great danger

I love education. I hold four degrees which shows my love of learning. I'm always reading and studying something new. I love the Scriptures and the freedom Christ brings. He enables us to have much higher and more powerful thoughts than we could generate on our own. There is, however, the great danger to intellectualized Christianity. By this I mean that we give mental assent to the concepts of Scripture, but our lives are not transformed by a living relationship with Jesus. It is easy for intellectual believers to get caught up in intellectualized truth rather than receiving revelation from God.

The hourglass problem

Our minds must be submitted to our spirit. When we make our mind the main thing, we bring enormous restriction to the life flow in our lives. It's a bit like an hourglass. At the center of the hourglass is a great restriction. If truth is represented by the grains of sand in the hourglass, then our minds represent the restriction in the middle. We have shown that God has downloaded truths into our inner being — into our human spirit. The danger we face is to intellectualize revelation. Let's not take each grain of truth and try to push it through our minds as the total arbiter of truth. Your spirit is a far more capable arbiter of truth than your intellect. Your spirit is being powered by Heaven and has capabilities that far exceed any extraordinary IQ. Your human spirit has the capacity to receive truth from God in an instant — all the grains of sand arriving at the same time. If, like me, you have a tendency to want to only accept the truth that your mind can fully understand, then you will be taking each grain of sand and pushing it through the tiny constriction of your mind — even if you have an excellent mind. This is the primary reason why so many intellectual believers grow so slowly. Their spiritual growth is hampered by the mind being the arbiter and regulator of truth.

This is what makes the Scriptures an even playing field for every believer. If this were not the case, then only smart believers would have revelation. Clearly this is not the case at all. In fact, intellectual believers often have the greatest difficulties with revelation because they have inadvertently created an hourglass problem in their inner being. The solution is to step out in faith and trust God for revelation that exceeds understanding. It is my experience that God in His great kindness will add understanding over time. If we wait for deeper and complete understanding of every truth before we act, we never act in faith but in our own strength. This is not the way of the Kingdom.

Please note that I am not saying the mind is bad and that intellectual pursuits are a waste of time. Not at all. I am saying that it is revelation that releases the life of God into our lives that causes transformation. Training our minds to be useful to God is a wonderful thing. For this to be effective, we have to teach our minds to set the truth of God's word as the primary source of authority. If we set ourselves up through our own intellects as the primary source of authority, we once again create the hourglass restriction. Jesus said He came to give us life and life in abundance. For that abundant life to flow, it must flow from our human spirit and saturate our inner world which includes saturating our minds with God's truth, His love and His ways.

This life was designed to be so simple that any child can do it and most children do. Jesus said that unless you become as a child you cannot access the Kingdom of God.

Enjoying your mind more

It is not that the Lord is against the mind. He would not tell us to renew our minds if He did not like them. What we will show in later chapters is that when the mind is ignited by the human spirit, it comes alive and is empowered to be way more creative, innovative and capable. It is not that God wants you to enjoy your mind less but that He wishes you to enjoy it more.

When Paul said that the weapons of our warfare are not carnal but mighty in God, he was being literal. Worldly thinking robs us from the life of God. We saw earlier that it darkens understanding and alienates us from God's life. The invitation of Scripture is that we allow God's thoughts to invade our thoughts and thereby allow His energizing life to flow into every aspect of our being.

5

CHAPTER FIVE

GOD'S FEELINGS ABOUT FEELINGS

One of the great gifts that God gives us is the ability to feel — to experience a wide range of emotions. This is what fundamentally connects us to our world and causes us to experience God's love. When we are afraid to feel we become afraid to live. It is sad that in some churches emotions are regarded with skepticism. We are not called to lead with our emotions in the same way we are not called to lead with our intellects. But God in His great kindness, has blessed us with the capacity to experience passion, love, joy, sadness, and a wide range of emotional responses.

As we develop the model further, we will find that in the same way the mind can be fed by the human spirit, so too can our emotions be fed. God is constantly streaming His love into our hearts. It is up to us to receive it. These godly emotions that begin in our inner core — our human spirit — are directly from God Himself. The Scripture says, "the joy of the Lord is our strength" (Nehemiah 8:10). Again we can clearly see that it is God's joy, not our joy, that is our strength. I find it fascinating that joy that originates in the spirit, overflows into our hearts and can even empower our physical bodies — give us strength. When we are sad or depressed we also feel depleted of physical energy.

Here we learn a great secret from David who wrote many of the Psalms. Almost all of David's Psalms go through the same stages. At first he expresses his feelings to God - and they are very human. He says things like "Hear my cry oh Lord," and, "How much longer, Lord?" David then accesses his human spirit and you see the transition in the Psalm.Words like, "but you O Lord are my strong fortress," and, "I will rejoice and be glad in you." It is interesting how David learned to strengthen himself in the Lord. He learned to encourage himself in God by proclaiming the truth about the Lord. You cannot become encouraged and find victory when you believe God is unfaithful and not good. When you start to declare the truth and align yourself with Heaven, you release all of Heaven's resources into your life.

That is why thanksgiving and praise are such powerful weapons. Praise moves your focus from your outer world and puts it on Jesus. We are speaking to the Lord who lives within us and not to an externalized God who is aloof and disinterested in our lives. We speak to our loving Father who has made His home in us. We speak the truth about who He is — that He's loving, kind, good, faithful, powerful, and wonderful.

All our emotions can be ignited

In the same way that we can access joy and peace, we can access compassion and love. Every passion and desire flows from our inner being out of our relationship with Jesus. The Scripture says God gives us the desires of our hearts, and by this it means that He places those desires there for us to enjoy. It does not mean that God wants to indulge our selfishness and our lusts. It means that powerful desires that are born in the heart of God, are being allocated to us. It means that God has set aside for you a human experience that is filled with love, joy and peace. He has placed things in your heart that move you deeply.

Often people want to understand their calling in life. One way to find out is to ask what breaks your heart. The things that move you very deeply, and that stir deep compassion or anger, are often aligned with God's call on your life. If you are angered by social injustice against those who cannot defend themselves, this is often a reflection of God's compassionate heart in you. Be very attentive to the things that break your heart and the things that stir you very deeply. These are the signposts of the desires that you've been given by your heavenly Father.

The great Christian writer and thinker, C. S. Lewis in his book The Weight of Glory, said, "It would seem that Our Lord finds our desires not too strong, but too weak. We are half-hearted creatures, fooling about with drink and sex and ambition when infinite joy is offered us, like an ignorant child who wants to go on making mud pies in a slum because he cannot imagine what is meant by the offer of a holiday at the sea. We are far too easily pleased."

The healing of wounds

Most people have been emotionally wounded in some way or another. In a large part it is simply a reality of living life with other people. Some have been very deeply wounded and feel they can never recover. But

Jesus is in the redemption business. He fully intends to bring wholeness and healing to every believer.

Intellectualized Christianity cannot bring such healing. Every person must experience God's love on a continual basis to find such healing and wholeness.

God thinks it's funny

I have experienced such extraordinary encounters with God. Very early on in my career, when I was in my mid-30s, I was leading a company that was pioneering a new technology in the insurance industry. One particular evening I was in a hotel in Dallas, Texas and I was under great stress. I had a meeting arranged with one of my customers the next morning which was very critical for our company. If we did not close this deal, the company and all its employees were at risk. The stress was tangible and I remember it well. It was about 10 pm that night and I could not sleep. While lying on my bed, I talked to the Lord about the situation. What happened next completely surprised me. The Lord put a picture in my mind of the size of my problem versus the enormity of His person. The juxtaposition of how puny my problem truly was versus how enormous and extraordinary He is, caused me to burst out laughing. The image got stronger and stronger and my laughter grew louder and louder. I laughed solidly for an hour until my stomach hurt. The joy of the Lord overwhelmed me and I was so refreshed when I woke up the next morning. I felt like a new man. The years of stress that had been built up and the feeling that I was carrying the world on my shoulders had all left. Jesus is a strong deliverer. (And yes, I did close the deal.)

Letting the things that break God's heart break yours

On another occasion I was traveling for business and arrived one afternoon in San Diego, California. A group of insurance executives were waiting for me downstairs. I decided to take a few minutes and pray before I went down — which is my habit. As I started praying I became very aware of the presence of the Lord and very quickly became overcome with His love for the lost (pre Christians). His compassion for those who do not know Him overwhelmed me. That compassion saturated my emotions and I wept and wept. It was a deep cry I could hardly explain. For the first time in my life I realized how deeply God loves people! I do not have the vocabulary or the writing expertise to convey to you how profound and deep that love is. But that afternoon I prayed like I've never prayed before. I called out to God for those in my life who did not know Him. Trust me when I say it was not a religious exercise but driven by a deep passion born in Heaven. I arrived at my meeting an hour late with very red eyes. It was difficult to focus on the business discussion because of the lingering emotion in my heart. I think it is true to say, that from that day on, I have had a deeper understanding of the love God has for people. That love has infected me. That experience — that download of compassion — transformed me.

It is impossible to walk with God and not experience His emotions. We know from the Scriptures that Jesus wept. We know that God laughs. We know that God experiences a wide range of emotion and that we have been created in His own image to experience those emotions too. Why would we create a theology that is emotionless — that deemphasizes experience and over emphasizes intellectualized truth? There is so much more in God than that.

I've seen many people emotionally healed from past wounds because of a powerful encounter with the Lord. Years of counseling can be saved through such encounters. I honor those people who have given themselves to counseling and to bringing those who are emotionally scarred to health and wholeness. It is a wonderful ministry indeed.

Once again, let us remember that our weapons are not carnal but mighty in God. We can tear down the lies on which many emotional wounds are built. We can help others experience God's love. It is a wonderful feeling to see people come to emotional healing and wholeness. I believe the most effective counseling involves connecting people directly to God's love and helping them to experience that reality.

Understanding our emotions brings liberty

The Lord intends our emotions to be informed by our human spirit. This is not a feel-good theology. We are talking about experiencing God's feelings. He means for us to enjoy all that He has for us. He loves to celebrate and it is time that we as the church learn to do the same. I love the fact that Jesus' first miracle involved giving people *more* wine at a party. I particularly like the fact that He provided a very large quantity of it and that the Scriptures go to great lengths to tell us exactly how much He provided — about 750 modern-day bottles of high quality wine. (By the way, Dr. Welsh invented a method of pasteurizing grape juice in 1869 so that fermentation was stopped, and the drink was non-alcoholic. He persuaded local churches to adopt this non-alcoholic "wine" for communion services, calling it "Dr. Welch's Unfermented Wine".) I wonder how many awards Jesus would win if he provided that wine today? I think it would win *World's Best Wine of the Year* at the very least.

Should we show emotion in church?

We do not have to be afraid of allowing people to express their emotions in church. There is a way to do it that is considerate to others. Most people may feel uncomfortable with such expressions and I can understand why. Somehow we have learned that church is a solemn place and that we need to show respect to God by being solemn and respectful. Perhaps we need to expand our view of God's emotions so we can expand our view of the church experience. Wouldn't it be strange if you attended a football game and everybody remained seated, solemn and respectful? At football games we expect people to be exuberant and to shout and applaud loudly. Culturally, we've given permission for such behavior in that context.

If we're that excited about our football team scoring, how much more excited should we be about the most wonderful Person in the universe? Is it possibly a matter of cultural permission? Perhaps we need to redefine our priorities? Church should be a place where people can express joy, receive compassion, be encouraged, express their sadness and feel comfortable doing so. After all, we are a family — the family of God. Surely families make space for one another to experience life, and church families make space for us to experience God.

A few years ago, such an event took place in our church. During the service, one particular woman began laughing uncontrollably. There was an awkwardness in the church. The pastor encouraged us to let her have her moment and to make space for her encounter. It was definitely an unusual experience for most people. A few days after the service, a group called me to discuss the matter. They decided that before they left the church they wished to discuss the inappropriateness of this sort of behavior in a church setting. At our meeting, one man said that he was offended by the laughter. I listened carefully for a while and asked the Lord for wisdom. He gave me a few questions to ask the group. So I said, "May I ask you, were you offended the previous week when that same woman was suffering with depression and she was crying in church? Did the spirit of depression upset you? Which spirit is offended by joy, the spirit of Jesus or a religious spirit?" I was amazed when the person leading the discussion looked at me and said, " Wow, I think I need to get rid of that religious spirit! How can I get offended with an expression of joy and not be offended by spirt of depression?" He got it. Those families stayed in the church.

If the church is going to be a place where people encounter God and come to wholeness, it means giving cultural permission for such encounters to be acceptable. It means that we may need to give up our neat orderly environments and make way for a little discomfort on our part for others to have wonderful encounters with the living God. Perhaps we have taken the idea of "meetings need to be in order" out of the context in which Paul meant them.

We have had situations where someone was having a powerful encounter with God and we moved them out of the main meeting into a side room where they could continue their encounter and not disrupt the main meeting. I am not advocating chaos but I am advocating church environments where people can encounter God's love. Such meetings can sometimes be a bit messy and we should be okay with that if we truly love people and care about their well-being.

It is time for us as believers to become offended by the destruction that the Kingdom of darkness is leveling against people. It is time for us to be offended and moved with compassion by the social injustice of our world. It is time for us to be emotionally touched by the problems of others and not just moved by our own problems. When we are willing to put the needs of others before our own, something extraordinary happens. We find we have resources that are supernaturally provided.

God takes care of your affairs as you take care of His

A few years ago my wife and I were invited to speak at a church in Texas. About a week before we were due to leave to minister, a serious crisis arose in our business. The logical and obvious thing to do was to cancel our trip to Texas and attend to the business. As we were praying about this, the Lord gave us a very clear word: "If you take care of My business I will take care of yours." So we stepped out in faith and found His resources were way more substantial than our own. About half way through the weekend of the ministry, I received a phone call from my business partner saying that the situation had dramatically changed. A large order that we were not expecting had come in! Jesus said, "Seek first the Kingdom of God and HIs righteousness and all these things will be added to you" (Matthew 6:33). It turns out He really means it. Our emotions can be quieted when we walk in obedience to Jesus.

People are in desperate need to live in the wholeness and fullness that God intended. If we are not willing to change our church services and our personal lifestyles to reach them, how will they experience God's love and encounter His beauty?

God is offering us a rich life filled with His emotions, His thoughts and His power. All we have to do is walk in them.

CHAPTER SIX

YOUR ETERNAL NATURE

We have now discussed the first two components of the human heart — mind and emotions. Before we discuss the next two — will and conscience - I want to share a powerful story with you that illustrates how a personal experience can dramatically change what you believe and think.

We may pursue our intellectual and academic studies our entire lives, but one experience with God can change our lives forever.

On November 10, 2008, at 4:30am, Eben Alexander woke up with tremendous back pain and shortly thereafter was admitted to the hospital as he slipped into a deep coma. Eben had contracted a rare form of meningitis that eats the glucose on the outer edges of the brain and then consumes brain cells. Dr. Eben Alexander is a well-regarded neurosurgeon and was a practicing neurosurgeon for 15 years at Harvard Medical School and associated hospitals. What Eben experienced was truly remarkable and shows that there is more to us than simply a body, a brain and learned neurological behaviors. This experience dramatically changed the neurosurgeon's life.

He describes his own beliefs as, "Although I considered myself a faithful Christian, I was more so in name than in actual belief. I didn't begrudge those who wanted to believe that Jesus was more than simply a good man who had suffered at the hands of the world. I sympathized deeply with those who wanted to believe that there was a God somewhere out there who loved us unconditionally. In fact, I envied such people the security that those beliefs no doubt provided. But as a scientist, I simply knew better than to believe them myself."

Eben remained in the coma for seven days during which he was virtually brain-dead. He describes his remarkable experience during the coma as having an earthworm like experience in which he was wading through mud and darkness in a very disturbing place. It all changed when a song moved him from that dark and muddy place and he found himself flying over a beautiful valley with millions of butterflies. It was a place of extraordinary beauty, he explains. In that place he had no words and his language was gone. In fact, he had no recollection of his life and no body awareness. Then he saw himself leaving this universe. He became aware that love was a huge part of the constituency of this place. He realized that it was all driven by a deep divine love and he became aware of a warm divine presence. He experienced unconditional love of an all-powerful, all-loving God and was completely overwhelmed by it. That overwhelming power brought him back to life.

At the end of the seven-day period, Dr. Alexander miraculously woke up much to the surprise of the medical staff, family and friends. He was bewildered by his experience. After his recovery, he set out to understand what had happened to him. He came up with several models of neuroanatomy and neurophysiology to describe it, but he could not come up with anything he felt adequately explained his experience.

Raymond Moody, M.D., Ph.D., author of *Life Beyond Life* commented on Eben's experience, saying, "Dr. Eben Alexander's near-death experience is the most astounding I have heard in more than four decades of studying this phenomenon. The circumstances of [Eben's] illness and his impeccable credentials make it very hard to formulate a mundane explanation for his case."

Alexander wrote about his life changing experience to Newsweek stating, "According to current medical understanding of the brain and mind, there is absolutely no way that I could have experienced even a dime with limited consciousness during my time in the coma, much less the hyper-vivid and completely coherent odyssey I underwent."

In his book, Proof of Heaven — *a neurosurgeon's journey into the afterlife,* Alexander wrote, 'there is no scientific explanation for the fact that while my body lay in coma, my mind — my conscious, inner self — was alive and well." He goes on to explain, "I'm still a doctor, and still a man of science every bit as much as I was before I had my experience. But on a deep level I'm very different from the person I was before, because I've caught a glimpse of this emerging picture of reality. And you can believe me when I tell you that it will be worth every bit of work it will take us, and those who come after us, to get it right."

He further asserts that the current understanding of the mind now lies broken at our feet, "What happened to me destroyed it, and I intend to spend the rest of my life investigating the true nature of consciousness and making the fact that we are more, much more, than our physical brains as clear as I can, both to my fellow scientists and to people at large."

Stories like this help us to understand that our human spirit is indeed the eternal part of who we are — the part that lives forever. It helps us see that it is also the most important part of who we are.

Needless to say the good doctor has come under significant attack. The scientific community insist that his experience was a brain-based delusion cobbled together by his synapses after they had somehow recovered. It is unlikely that the mainstream medical community will accept Eben's explanation. No matter what he says, it can always be construed as his personal and subjective experience unsubstantiated by scientific and medical knowledge.

The purpose of telling the story was not to prove anything medically or scientifically, but to show how one experience can dramatically alter the course of one's life. Because these experiences occur in the spiritual realm, they are nearly impossible to prove at the intellectual level.

Sharing spiritual experiences

When you try to "prove" your God experiences, you are almost certainly setting yourself up for failure. There is, however, a far more effective way to share such experiences: remember that your audience has a human spirit too.

I found in my own professional career, it is far more effective to share my spiritual experiences openly rather than attempt to "prove" them. Critics may claim that they are nothing but subjective, delusional and self induced hallucinations.

Most people are very interested in hearing about such experiences. The reason is that the human spirit bears witness with the truth of what is being shared. Anyone listening to a spiritual experience will be drawn to it as the Holy Spirit confirms it to their spirit.

Often the Holy Spirit uses these stories to open people's hearts to the supernatural. It may cost professional credibility and, in an extreme case, your career. But God never takes anything from us without replacing it with something far greater and far more wonderful. History is full of professional people who were believers who have had extraordinary experiences.

I have learned to trust the Lord and be vulnerable with the stories. Deep down every person — believer or not — knows that there is more to life than the physical world. This explains our cultures obsession with aliens, fantasy stories and superheroes. We love the idea that some people may have superhuman abilities. We are more than just entertained by it, we are drawn to it because something deep within us bears witness with the supernatural realm.

Without supernatural power, Christianity is reduced to a set of laws and a list of principles. But God is not contained by human philosophies and externalized religion. He is the creator of the universe and the lover of our souls. Every human being on the planet has been designed to have a relationship with Him. We, therefore, do not need to be embarrassed about the gospel. We can confidently and openly share God's love, and His powerful dealings with human beings, with any person we meet.

Everyone has a spirit

Think how much more powerful the human spirit is: It is the very core of your being — your inner being, and the essence of your personhood. Some movies that we watch move us in our emotions or our intellects, but some movies touch us more deeply — they go beyond just our human emotions and touch the very core of our being.

There is something very powerful about the human spirit and when that part of us is ignited we feel very much alive. When we share stories of what God has done it causes people to come alive. The deepest part of them is stirred.

When we are born again, our spirit man is made alive to God. Once we were dead in our sins and in our transgressions, we believed on the Lord Jesus Christ and a spectacular miracle took place. We went from death to life, from an object of wrath to a beloved child, and we became a new creation. In some ways we become more than human because now we are in-dwelt by the eternal God - a perfectly loving being that has taken up residence in our inner man. What a mind blowing concept.

Spiritual things are easily understood by your human spirit. Truths that your spirit understands intuitively may take many years for your mind to understand.

Think about this for a minute. This part of you has enormous capacity — it is so great that it can have fellowship with an eternal God! This eternal Being that spoke the universe into existence now takes residence in your inner man. What extraordinary capabilities your spirit has to make that possible.

The Kingdom of God is a spiritual kingdom. It is a kingdom that goes beyond time and space, and the only way for us to live in it is to be born of the Spirit and be made alive to God. When you came to Jesus this dramatic transformation happened to you. You were born into a new realm — the Kingdom of God. And in this new realm, you have a faculty to interact and live in this astonishing place.

The kingdom works very differently than our natural world. We are all given a human spirit with the capacity to fellowship with an eternal God, and that capacity is so enormous and so capable that it dwarfs any intelligence or other capability.

CHAPTER SEVEN

YOUR WILL BE DONE

Going back to the study of the *heart*, we want to look at the next component — the *will*. A great deal of theology has been dedicated to the discussion of man's free *will*. We are going to allow the Scripture to teach us how the will works and how we can know God's *will*.

This is a wonderful topic that can truly transform your life when you understand that God has designed you to enjoy abundant life **now** — not just in Heaven one day.

Your free will

When the disciples asked Jesus to teach them how to pray, He taught them that famous prayer we all know so well. Here is the prayer as it occurs in Matthew 6:9-13

Our Father who is in Heaven,
Hallowed be your name.
Your kingdom come,
your will be done,
on Earth, as it is in Heaven.
Give us this day our daily bread,
and forgive us our debts,
as we also have forgiven our debtors.
And lead us not into temptation,
but deliver us from evil.

Notice verse 10, "Your kingdom come, your will be done, on Earth as it is in Heaven." How is God's will done in Heaven? Are people in Heaven free? Are people in Heaven capable of making their own decisions? The answer to this is the key to understanding how we too can be free.

People in Heaven are aligned with God's will and are therefore free to choose. The same is true for us, when we are lined up with the will of God we are free to choose.

Your *will* is that part of your heart which causes you to make choices and be purposeful. It is informed by the world (the flesh) or by Heaven through your spirit. There is no independent *will*. It turns out that you're only truly free when you are in Christ. Galatians 5:1 says, "It is for freedom that Christ set you free." Jesus is all about freedom. He desires you to be truly free. He paid an extraordinary price for your freedom.

When you are bound up in sin you're not free — you're bound. And when you're a slave to sin, your *will* is informed by sinful desires and purposes. Paul talks about this in Ephesians 2:3 when he says, "All of us also lived among them at one time, gratifying the cravings **[will]** of our flesh and following its desires and thoughts. Like the rest, we were by nature deserving of wrath." This word "cravings" is the word *will* — the same word Jesus used when He said, "your *will* be done".

This will is not your *will* but the *will* of the world and its sinful ways trying to impose its purposes and *will* for your life on you. Jesus broke that control at the cross. He broke the power of sin and death over you so that you are no longer a slave to sin and you are no longer subject to the *will* of sin.

To remind you of our previous discussion about the flesh, evil does not reside in physical matter. Paul uses the word flesh when we allow our bodies to be a gateway for sin's control in our lives. When we do this we are behaving as unbelievers who are still subject to the control and the will of sin.

But we are free in Jesus. We are no longer subject to sin and its will. We are now free to choose. That is why Jesus said that He did not come to do His own will but to do that of His Father. Jesus was saying that His will was informed by His Father and not by the world. These are the only two choices. The great deception is when we believe that there is a third option. There is no independent will that can function on its own. Either my will — like Jesus - is informed by Heaven, or it is informed by the world. Once my will is aligned with God's will I find real freedom.

I know this sounds counterintuitive since worldly thinking tells us that when we're not subject to anyone else's will, then we are free. This is a powerful deception and simply not true. What the world calls "free" is in fact bondage designed to keep us under the control of sin and keep our lives substantially restricted by what the Kingdom of darkness wills. Jesus liberated us from the prison of the world system and has translated us into a new world under His Lordship. In that new place, we have become citizens of Heaven and are now free.

God's will is a very broad, free and liberating place. The kingdom of darkness can offer nothing but restriction, depletion, reduction and ultimately destruction.

When we live with a free will - one set free by Jesus - we find our purpose in life. We find that we are free to pursue our true calling. We find why we were made and we begin to choose accordingly.

Moving to America

The best way to illustrate this is to tell you the story of how we moved to America. In December 1992, I was in Munich Germany on a business trip. I arrived about seven hours before my clients and as I walked into my hotel room I became aware of an intense sense of the presence of the Lord. I threw my bags on the bed, pulled out my Bible and Journal, and began to write.

One of the clearest things I heard in my spirit that morning was that we were to move to Atlanta, Georgia in the United States. What makes this so unusual is that I had never had a desire to go to America or to even visit. South Africans tend to be Eurocentric in their thinking having been a British colony until 1961. What was more amazing was that I was not aware that Atlanta was a city and that Georgia was a state and that the two were related. This was before the Internet so it took several days until I was in a position to find a map and I was delighted to find there was such a place as Atlanta Georgia! I had no idea what Georgia was like or what it meant to live there.

So why did God have to tell me this in such clear terms? I believe the reason is what happened a few days later. The CEO of the German company offered me the opportunity to be president of his company and move to Germany. It was truly an incredible offer and a very generous one! God got in first and made sure that I knew His will before I received the compelling offer. A worldly mindset would see a generous financial offer as God's will. In this case, it was not.

A few days later I arrived back in South Africa and shared my experience with Bridget. I found that God had prepared her heart too. We decided not to share this information with our business partners or anyone else until God confirmed this in His way and in His time. A few weeks after my return, I was praying with several of my business partners when one of them said, "I have a strong sense that you are going to go somewhere — somewhere unexpected — like America." I shared very briefly with my partners what had happened but I was careful not to mention Atlanta in my explanation.

I was amazed with the transformation that began in my heart since that hotel encounter. God was making me aware of the desires and purposes He had planted in my heart. I found myself developing a love for America - a country that I had never been to and about which I knew very little. When God calls you, He gives you His love for the place and for the people. On my drive to work in the morning from Pretoria to Johannesburg every day, I found myself praying for the country and for the city of Atlanta. The more I prayed the more my heart was stirred.

In 1993, I visited the USA with a business partner who had decided to move with us. He had lived in America before and was 20 years my senior. That first morning we landed in New York and took our connecting flight to Atlanta. We visited 13 cities in 10 days and visited some friends in Orange County, California. Before the end of the trip, my partner suggested that we return to Atlanta one more time, and as the plane landed on the runway at Hartsfield International Airport, he turned to me and said, "This just feels right." I smiled and he immediately became suspicious and asked, "You've known all along haven't you?" I shared the remaining details of my hotel encounter and the very specific call to Atlanta.

I share this story to show that our minds can be renewed when we are tuned in to the Spirit of the Lord. In this process we came to know God's will. A renewed mind knows God's will. Paul confirms this idea in Romans 12:2 when he instructs us, "Do not conform to the pattern of this world, but be transformed by the renewing of your mind. Then you will be able to test and approve what God's will is--his good, pleasing and perfect will."

This transformation happens when we seek God - when we allow our minds to be informed by our spirit and allow the Holy Spirit to connect us with the mind of Christ. We then choose to do His will and this always leads us to freedom. We chose His will — not out of a sense of obligation or dutiful drudgery — but out of a joyful response to the newly discovered desires in our hearts that He placed there. We can do what Ephesians 6:6 says, "... doing the will of God from your heart."

I'd love to tell you that everything went smoothly once we arrived in Atlanta. It was a difficult adjustment to become accustomed to another culture. But the one thing that never changed was our certainty that we were called to the city and to serve these people. God wants us to stand firm in His will. He wants us to be fully assured as Paul says in Colossians 4:12 "... that you may stand firm in all the will of God, mature and fully assured."

There is much to love about the South - the people are kind, courteous, generous and Southern cuisine can be very addictive — bring on the shrimp and grits! After about 10 years, we settled down and began to fall in love with the place we now called home. We have been blessed with an extraordinary community and a wonderful church family. Since we arrived in Atlanta we helped plant a church, we started a school, and created several businesses. It is now hard to imagine living anywhere else. Through all the ups and downs of cultural adjustments, acclamation to the business environment, adjustment to the spiritual atmosphere, we remained anchored in the fact that we were called to Atlanta Georgia. We knew it was God's will for us.

No jurisdiction

Imagine for a minute that the South African police arrived at my home in Atlanta Georgia and they demanded payment of South African taxes. As an American citizen, I'm subject to American taxes and American law. No matter how convinced the South African authorities may be, their claim is irrelevant since they have no jurisdiction in the United States. I owe no allegiance or taxes to South Africa. I'm not subject to South African law any longer.

When you came to Christ you changed jurisdiction. You are no longer under the Jurisdiction of sin. You are free to live in your new country in Christ.

As simple as the previous example is, many believers still think they are subject to the laws of sin. They are not! Imagine if I was unclear about jurisdiction when the South African police arrived at my door. Perhaps I'd allow them to arrest me and even imprison me and make all sorts of demands on me and my family. Similarly, if you are unclear as a believer, that you are now free from the law of sin and death and are now only subject to Christ, then you will allow sin in your life to make demands, imprison you, and impose its will on your life. We will show in a later chapter that you are truly free from sin and the only jurisdiction that you are now subject to is the law of Christ.

The law of Christ is an extremely broad place full of life, freedom and exceptional fulfillment. Before you came to Jesus, you in fact, had no choice — you were under the jurisdiction of sin. Now that you are in Jesus, you can choose to live free.

It is fascinating that the enemy makes demands on believers, and surprisingly believers submit themselves to these demands — claiming they have no choice. What an extraordinary deception that enables the enemy to play on the ignorance of believers.

Don't be foolish

The Bible tells us, "Do not be foolish, but understand what the Lord's will is" (Ephesians 5:17). This word "understand" means to *join the dots* and to get it. When we don't "get it" the Bible calls this foolishness. Now this would be a very unkind thing for Paul to say if it were beyond our ability to *get it*. The reason that Paul is saying this is because God's will is being streamed to your heart from your spirit constantly — from the fountain of life within.

It is interesting that Jesus used this word often asking people, "Do you not understand?" He showed frustration with their lack of understanding. We know that Jesus is kind, patient and loving, so this must mean that what He was saying was well within their ability to understand or he would not have been frustrated with how dull they were — how foolish they were. He even became frustrated with His own disciples when they did not "get it."

One of the capabilities of your heart is to become clear about the will of God in your life. Worldly thinking creates a darkness in your mind and an inability to know God's will. This is what Paul calls *foolishness*. We will discuss this supernatural capability to "get it" later in the book.

Practically, how can I know God's will?

Jesus has fully qualified you before the Father. Because of Jesus, you come to the Father boldly knowing that you are fully acceptable to Him. There needs to be no hesitation on your part in asking the Father for anything. Jesus encouraged us to ask the Father for anything in His name.

1. God's general will

What I mean by God's general will, is that there are things that God wills for all His sons and daughters. As an example, "It is God's will that you should be sanctified: that you should avoid sexual immorality" (1 Thessalonians 4:3). It is God's will that we love one another deeply from the heart. It is God's will that we, "Go into all the world and preach the gospel to all creation" (Mark 16:15). It is God's will that "... you may live a life worthy of the Lord and please him in every way: bearing fruit in every good work, growing in the knowledge of God" (Colossians 1:10).

You can know God's general will by studying the Scriptures and by attending a Bible-based church.

2. God's specific will for you

A. <u>God provides Purpose.</u> God's specific will for you is based on His call on your life. Every one of us has a purpose in God - a specific call that is His will for our lives. This purpose is your contribution to the world and the reason for which you were born. When you start doing it, everything in you proclaims, "I was born to do this!" You were design to love doing what you were called to do. This does not mean it will be easy but it will be very meaningful. There are specific things that God has set aside for you. In fact, the Scripture says that God has gone before you and prepared every good work for you to walk in. Look at what He says in Ephesians

2:10, "For we are His workmanship, created in Christ Jesus for good works, which God prepared beforehand that we should walk in them."

B. God provides Pointers. God provides pointers for you to help you identify this specific call on your life - this purpose. We talked earlier about being aware of the things that break your heart and the things that cause you to become righteously indignant. When your emotions respond in this particular way, it is often because your heart is being informed by your spirit according to God's will for your life. When we tune in to the things that are in our spirit, we become aware of passions and desires that God has planted there. I'm not saying that every passion and desire is from God, because some of these may be worldly and not informed by your spirit. Another pointer is to observe your gifts and abilities. God has equipped you with everything you need to do His will and that is why He says in Hebrews 13:21, "God will equip you with everything good for doing his will, and may he work in us what is pleasing to him, through Jesus Christ, to whom be glory for ever and ever. Amen." So, by studying how God has equipped you, you can discover what He has equipped you to do.

C. God provides People. Part of God's kindness to us is to provide us with leaders, mentors, and other people of influence who can help us to understand God's will for our lives. If you do not have such a person in your life, pray right now that the Lord would provide you a mentor. You'd be amazed at how God does this. It may require you to boldly approach someone in your church or your community. When God provides you with such a mentor, He puts it in their hearts too. Do not be worldly in how you approach this. Put your faith in God and ask Him to bring you such a person. Do not worry about what the mentor may think — in this you can trust God to move their hearts.

D. <u>God provides Practically.</u> Start by serving in your local church. Many believers are waiting for God to supernaturally call them into their ministry before they begin to do anything. I've heard business people say that when they've made enough money they are going to serve God full-time. You will find that God does not work this way. Once you pour yourself into serving in your local church, He opens the way and you begin walking in your ministry. We are all in the ministry. Some get paid by a business, some by a church and some by a non-profit organization. Regardless of how you are paid, you can be in full time ministry in your job.

This is like getting in a car. Starting the engine, pointing it in a certain direction, and begin driving. As the car is moving forward, God helps you steer it in the right direction — even if you started off pointing in the wrong direction.Start serving where there is need in the church (or in the community) and God will lead you.

The second practical aspect of finding God's will for your life, is to start giving financially into the area that you believe God is leading you into. Jesus said, "Where your treasure is there your heart will be also." This means that you can steer your heart by what you give to. The more you give to a specific cause the more your heart will belong to it. Again, it is my experience that believers often want their heart to belong to something first and then they will give to it — completely the wrong way around. When we sow in faith we reap in joy. The bottom line is: start where you are, talk to others, give generously, and serve faithfully. As you take on responsibility God will complement you by giving you more responsibility. Responsibility is indeed a reward from the Lord. Focus on responsibility not authority. People who grab for authority are a danger in the church. You do not have to reach for authority but simply receive it. God will provide you with the necessary authority that you need to achieve the responsibility He has assigned to you.

Do not wait for someone to invite you to do something meaningful. Step out in faith, trust God, and get on with it.

E. God provides Promises. As you persevere you will receive all that God has promised. "You need to persevere so that when you have done the will of God, you will receive what he has promised" (Hebrews 10:36). Promises are the currency of Heaven. As you begin to step out and walk in God's will for your life, He will give you many promises specific to your ministry and to your life. God gives us promises so that we will enlarge our vision, persevere during difficult times, and ultimately receive all that He has promised. Promises expand us and cause us to be aligned with Heaven. There will be specific Bible verses that will serve as your life promises — these are specific promises from God that define your purpose and calling. If you do not have life promises, ask God to give them to you. Remember these have been deposited in your spirit by the Lord, and He can reveal them to you anytime you ask.

You will be delighted with the will of God for your life just like Peter speaks about in 1 Peter 4:2, "As a result, they do not live the rest of their earthly lives for evil human desires, but rather for the will of God."

There is truly nothing more fulfilling in life than doing what you know you were called to do. You know those moments when you find your "grace zone." God has put a mechanism in your spirit that will bear witness when you do the thing you are designed to do.

You know the feeling well. It causes you to shout out, "I was born for this!"

CHAPTER EIGHT

ENJOYING A CLEAR CONSCIENCE

We come now to the last part of our discussion of the human heart — the *conscience*. We have seen that our human spirit, when inhabited by God, becomes the fountain of life within. We have seen how this fountain can inform our minds, ignite our emotions and empower our will. In the same way, our conscience can either be informed by our spirit (led by the Holy Spirit) or by external factors.

Many believers live in a constant state of low grade condemnation. It seems that their conscience is constantly accusing them. This does not line up with Scripture that says, "Therefore, there is now no condemnation for those who are in Christ Jesus" (Romans 8:1).

The Bible encourages us to draw near to God with sincere heart, and full assurance that faith brings. By faith our hearts were sprinkled by the blood of Christ which cleansed us from a guilty conscience, as it says in Hebrews 10:22, "let us draw near to God with a sincere heart and with the full assurance that faith brings, having our hearts sprinkled to cleanse us from a guilty conscience and having our bodies washed with pure water."

Keep what you were given

When you came to Christ, He cleansed you from all unrighteousness (1 John 1:9), and He cleansed you from a guilty conscience too. Your job is to keep the gift you were given. You are to <u>keep</u> your conscience clear. This is what Paul told Timothy, "They must **keep hold** of the deep truths of the faith <u>with a clear conscience</u>" (1 Timothy 3:9).

Believers who do not understand how to keep their conscience clear seem to struggle their whole lives with the feeling that they are not right with God. It is like an internal voice that disqualifies them from spiritual blessing and intimacy with God.

Paul's story

In its early days, the church faced powerful persecution. Among the worst things the church had to endure was watching leaders and other members being killed for the sake of the gospel. There was one mastermind that drove this initiative - Saul. This

Pharisee was relentless and his aim was to wipe out this disease called Christianity from the face of the Earth. He implemented his plan skillfully until one day he had a power encounter with Jesus which dramatically changed his life. He became known as Paul the apostle.

Fortunately for Paul, his salvation included a fresh clean conscience. Imagine if the apostle Paul could never get over his past and forgive himself for what he had done to the church and to those early believers. But once he received forgiveness, he also received the cleansing of his conscience. From that day on he endeavored to keep his conscience clear. It is amazing how many times Paul talks about his conscience throughout the New Testament. This is coming from a guy who had Christians killed.

In Acts 24:16 he says, "So I strive always to **keep** my conscience clear before God and man." In Romans 9:1 he says, "I speak the truth in Christ--I am not lying, my conscience **confirms it through the Holy Spirit.**"

A conscience governed by the Holy Spirit

You are free from your conscience being governed by your past. You are free from your conscience being governed by the old covenant law (more about this later). You are free from your conscience being governed by your culture. You are now free to have your conscience governed by the Holy Spirit. Your conscience does not have to be informed by your past, your failures, your church tradition, or your culture.

If you had been strategically killing people — thinking that you were serving God - as Paul did — you would have to master this idea of a cleansed conscience to be able to live and function normally as a person. For Paul, this wasn't a matter of spiritual maturity, but a matter of being able to function normally. He discovered the secret that his conscience was not to be informed by worldly thinking but informed by the Holy Spirit - by God's grace. His human spirit (in fellowship with the Holy Spirit) informed his conscience. Look carefully at what he says in 2 Corinthians 1:12, "Now this is our boast: Our **conscience testifies** that we have conducted ourselves in the world, and especially in our relations with you, with integrity and godly sincerity. We have done so, relying not on worldly wisdom but on God's grace."

Your pledge to stay free

When we come to Christ, we make a public declaration of our decision to follow Jesus by being baptized in water. This action declares that we were once dead in our sins, were buried with Christ and we were raised in newness of life in him.

It was also a pledge to keep our conscience clear before the Lord. Peter reminds us of this in 1 Peter 3:21, "and this water symbolizes baptism that now saves you also--not the removal of dirt from the body but the **pledge of a clear conscience toward God.** It saves you by the resurrection of Jesus Christ."

The big red button

Imagine a counter that clocks up every time we commit a sin. As the sinning continues, the condemnation grows, the shame builds, the counter rises higher and higher. One day we encounter Christ and our lives are transformed forever. On that day Jesus hits the big red reset button on your conscience. He resets it to zero. No longer can the past accuse you and cause you shame.The counter has been reset and all its previous entries forgotten and forgiven.

You still have the same conscience but reset — cleansed. Now your conscience needs to be informed by the Lord and not by the things that previously informed it before you came to Christ. The things that caused it to count before have been canceled. Those things have been replaced by a person — the Holy Spirit.

Your job is to keep the counter at zero. When the wrong things influence your conscience you can remind yourself that Christ hit the big red reset button and that you are no longer condemned.

Sin and condemnation

When the woman who was discovered in adultery was brought to Jesus, we see a fascinating sequence of events. My first thought is, where was the guy that was involved in this, and why was he not brought to Jesus? My next question is: who found them in bed and why were the Pharisees so quickly informed? Well, any answer to these questions is pure speculation. What we do know is that the Pharisees tried to use this to trap Jesus. They knew that He understood the law required her to be stoned. If He agreed that she should be stoned, then His message of forgiveness was discredited. If He did not have her stoned then He was guilty of breaking the law and they would have a basis to accuse Him. We know that He invited those who had not sinned to throw the first stone, and everyone left until it was just Jesus and the woman remaining. He asked the woman, "Where are your accusers?" She said, "There are none." Jesus was showing her that accusation had left her life. He then reinforced it with His own authority and said, "Neither do I condemn you. Go and sin no more."

This is a fantastic example of how a true conscience in Christ works. When people feel condemned and accused they will continue to sin. When people are free from condemnation and accusation then they are in a position to go and sin no more. I wonder how many times we have misrepresented Christ as the church when we've insisted that if people will "sin no more" and then we will not condemn them — completely backwards.

Here is the story: "Jesus straightened up and asked her, 'Woman, where are they? Has no one condemned you?' 'No one, sir,' she said. 'Then neither do I condemn you,' Jesus declared. 'Go now and leave your life of sin'"(John 8:10-11 NIV).

Helping others with their conscience

Paul explained to the Corinthians that some people have a weak conscience and that we should not offend or wound a weak conscience. "When you sin against them in this way and wound their weak conscience, you sin against Christ" (1 Corinthians 8:12). "I am referring to the other person's conscience, not yours. For why is my freedom being judged by another's conscience?" (1 Corinthians 10:29)

In Christ we're made completely free and have had our conscience cleared. Some believers have not fully accepted the fact that the price of their sin has been fully paid by Christ. They are in the process of understanding what truly happened at the cross on their behalf. This results in them being burdened with restrictions that seek to govern their lives — stuff that Jesus paid for to set them free — but the same stuff that still holds them under restriction. Paul calls this a "weak" conscience. We are instructed to be loving towards those who have a weak conscience and not to wound the conscience by indulging our freedom at their expense. Paul goes on to say that if we do this we sin against Christ.

What informs your conscience?

"This is the covenant I will establish with the people of Israel after that time, declares the Lord. I will put my laws in their minds and write them on their hearts. I will be their God, and they will be my people. ... For I will forgive their wickedness and will remember their sins no more". By calling this covenant 'new,' he has made the first one obsolete; and what is obsolete and outdated will soon disappear" (Hebrews 8:10, 12-13 NIV).

Notice the last part of the verses we just read. It says that the new covenant with Christ has caused the old covenant to be **obsolete** and **outdated**. Our conscience is not governed by the law of the old covenant but by the law of the Spirit. When God writes His laws in our hearts and minds, these are the laws that come from our inner being — the fountain of life within. It is our human spirit indwelled by God that writes laws on our hearts. We are no longer governed by externalized religion of the old covenant law, but by the law of the Spirit fed from within our human spirit.

This was a big debate during the early church and Paul fought furiously for the freedom of believers to ensure that that they did not submit themselves again to the old covenant laws. He explained that the law was simply a guardian until Christ came so that we can then be justified by faith. Once Christ came there was no more need for the law-guardian.

He argued this point in Galatians 3:21, 24-25, "Is the law, therefore, opposed to the promises of God? Absolutely not! For **if** a law had been given that could impart life, then righteousness would certainly have come by the law. ... So the law was our guardian **until Christ came** that we might be justified by faith. Now that this faith has come, we are no longer under a guardian."

Your conscience is now governed by the law of the Spirit of life. Your life is regulated by this Spirit-led conscience, "because through Christ Jesus the law of the Spirit who gives life has set you free from the law of sin and death" (Romans 8:2).

Enjoying a clear conscience

You will find that the Holy Spirit will lead you in the path of the righteousness that Jesus has imparted to you. At no point will the Holy Spirit lead you to contradict the Scriptures. Our salvation is true freedom in Christ and not a license for sin or irresponsible behavior.

God does not endorse destructive choices

He is fiercely committed to loving you and bringing you into the freedom for which He paid so dearly. He is not interested in fixing externalized religion with its list of rules and its observations. He wants you to have a vital living relationship with Him. He has given you everything you need to live a life of godliness. He activates the fountain of life to flow constantly and overflow into every area of your life.

The Holy Spirit is now the sole means for regulating your life, your character, and your behavior.

The Daniel vow

As you learn to live in freedom, the Holy Spirit may place restrictions on your life. Things that other believers may do will be prohibited for you. We see this in the life of Daniel. Daniel and his friends had been taken into captivity and forced to serve a heathen king. During this time, the King gave explicit instructions to feed Daniel and his friends with choice foods and the best wine. But Daniel's conscience was informed by the Lord and he asked that he only be given water and vegetables. This was an act of faith and Daniel created alignment between his life and Heaven. We can call this a "Daniel vow".

Sometimes, the Holy Spirit will bring restriction to your life for your own good. It may be to protect you, or to ensure that others do not have access to your life that could be damaging or harmful to you. At these times, your obedience to these restrictions are vital. God may even require from you a Daniel vow.

In my mid-20s, while serving at a large church in South Africa as the youth pastor, I remember speaking with the senior pastor about this concept. He told me that he loved real estate and if he had not been called to the ministry he would have built a large real estate portfolio. He shared that God had required from him a restriction: not to be involved in real estate, but to be focused on the ministry. The Lord said that if he did that, the Lord would grow the ministry for him. That church became one of the most influential churches in the nation. Real estate investments are fine for every other believer, but not for this pastor. It was his Daniel vow not to do so. There is no Scripture prohibiting him from doing so — just his conscience being informed by the Holy Spirit. One wonders what would have happened if he had not kept his Daniel vow.

I once had the fortunate blessing to have a leader of a movement visit us in our home. At that time, the movement had several thousand churches in over 40 countries. I was amazed to discover that the leader of the movement also had a Daniel vow. The Lord had asked him to always "step aside" and never to make himself the focus of attention, and that if he did that, the Lord would grow the movement.

I hesitate to put this in writing, but I too have a Daniel vow. From that early encounter in Munich Germany, God has made it clear to me that I am not to be the CEO of anyone else's company but my own. I have been blessed with spectacular offers which I have declined for the sake of my commitment to the Lord. There is absolutely nothing wrong with being the CEO of someone else's company. In fact, I hire senior executives who are believers and I'm very thankful that they are willing to lead our organizations. But in my particular case, my conscience is informed by the Lord - not by the law — not by religious tradition — not by some leader — but by the Holy Spirit in my inner being.

There are no islands just family

This is the new offer of life in Christ: we can live free with our lives regulated directly by the Holy Spirit. As part of this regulation, God puts leaders around us to whom we must submit and be accountable.

It is possible to sear your conscience to the point that you can no longer hear God. "The Spirit clearly says that in later times some will abandon the faith and follow deceiving spirits and things taught by demons. Such teachings come through hypocritical liars, whose consciences have been seared as with a hot iron" (1 Timothy 4:1-2 NIV).

This is the reason that we are a part of a family of believers. As leaders, it is our responsibility to watch over others as people who must give an account to God. We need to watch our own lives and hold others accountable to the grace of God in theirs.

Gentle correction is a normal and everyday part of life in the body of Christ. That's why Paul says in Galatians 6:1-3, "Brothers and sisters, if someone is caught in a sin, you who live by the Spirit should restore that person gently. But watch yourselves, or you also may be tempted. Carry each other's burdens, and in this way you will fulfill the law of Christ. If anyone thinks they are something when they are not, they deceive themselves."

From this chapter, you can see that an extraordinary miracle took place the day you came to Christ: your conscience was cleared. When you believe that Jesus paid the price in full, you no longer feel that you still need to pay. This freedom liberates you to follow the law of life in Jesus Christ.Your safeguard is to belong to a vibrant church where you can serve and where the leaders watch over you in a gentle way. There are no islands in Christ only family!

CHAPTER NINE

WHAT REALLY HAPPENED AT THE CROSS?

It was the dawn of mankind. In a world of perfection and unspeakable beauty, man had been given a home — a perfect place to live out an exuberant, joy-filled life. It is difficult to imagine what a perfect place it was — a place of no sin, no pain, no injustice, no tears, no sadness, no hurt and no disappointment. In this place, mankind could fulfill every purpose for which it was created and find deep meaning, perfect intimacy and an ecstatic lifestyle.

Our story picks up a few hours after the fall of mankind. Adam and Eve have just done what they were told not to do. They were given a simple choice: to keep what God had given them or to believe a lie and give it all up. The enemy had just used one of his two standard deceptions which he has used for all mankind since. The first deception is to question God's word by asking, "did God really say?" The second is to question their true identity. The enemy did this to get them to give up what God had already freely given them. The strategy was simple: He asked the woman, "Did God really say, 'you must not eat from any tree in the garden'?" God did indeed say they could eat from any tree except from the tree in the middle of the garden. "You'll certainly not die" the enemy said to the woman, "God knows that when you eat from it your eyes will be opened and you will be like God, knowing good and evil."

Her husband was with her and said nothing. He was standing right there and did nothing to stop it — the first act of male wimpishness. They both ate and their eyes were indeed opened but they did not become like God. They chose to believe a lie about God's true motives and about their true identity in Him - an astounding moment in human history so inconceivable, and the consequences so unbearable!

The Godhead meeting

Imagine the meeting among the Godhead in that moment:
Jesus turns to the Father with great sadness in His heart and says, "It is as you said Father - they have sinned."
The Father turns to His beloved Son and replies with a depth of love in His voice, "It is time Son. The only way this can change is to do what we planned before the beginning of time."
"I will go Father. I will lay down my life for them that they may have eternal life and be reunited to us in love."
The Father turned to the Holy Spirit and said, "They need to learn that they need a Savior - before the Son lays down His life for them. Give them a Guardian — the Law and show them they are incapable of keeping the Law and when they fail at all their attempts, they will come to understand that they need a Savior and that their own self righteousness will never redeem them."
The Holy Spirit stares knowingly into the Father's eyes, "I will do as you say Father. I will find prophets among them and I will give them the Law and prepare the way for Jesus."

Jesus thoughtfully interjects, "You know Father, even when I pay for their sins and redeem them back to us, they will still sin."

"Yes," He answers, "then we will give them a new nature that is part of ours so that they can participate in our divine nature. We will make them one with us."

Jesus adds with sadness, "Yes, Father. But they will still sin".

The Father rises to His feet, loudly and powerfully declares, "Then we shall take an oath that we will never hold their sin against them again. All sin will be put on you, Son, and you will pay for their sin once for all — breaking the power of sin and death over their lives forever!" There is triumphant agreement in the Godhead! "And we will take residence in them, making them one with us that they may know the pure ecstasy of our love and our intimacy." The Father continues, "Even so, they will need someone to guide them and to lead them into all truth."

Immediately the Holy Spirit volunteers, "I will go and be their Guide and lead them into all truth. I will be their Comforter and their Counselor. I will show them Jesus and the beauty of His person that they may be the Bride you prepared for Him Father."

The Father confirms the Holy Spirit's plan, "And you precious Holy Spirit will be the power of the church and equip the beautiful Bride for the Son. She will be spotless and without sin — not by her own doing but by the perfect sacrifice of the Son. We will give her the gift of righteousness and she will be holy and blameless".

After a little thought, the Father adds, "I will give each of them grace gifts so that each one will play a role as they learn to love and to serve one another just as we do. I'll go before them and prepare every good deed for them to walk in. And you my precious Holy Spirit, will guide them so that they may know the purpose of their lives and that to which we have called them." The Father turns to the Son with great joy in His face and declares, "And you my dear Son shall have your Bride - beautiful, perfect and in permanent union with us." The Godhead breaks into great celebration and singing. The plan is in motion!

Before the world began

Every aspect of this story is an element of Scripture. The Scriptures teach that before the foundations of the world, Jesus planned to lay His life down at the cross to redeem His Bride. Revelation 13:8 says, "the Lamb was slain from the creation of the world." The Bible goes on to say that before the foundations of the world the Father loved the Son and gave Him glory (John 17:24).

Isn't that incredible? What love God has for us!

You were in God's mind before time was created, as it says in Ephesians 1:4. "as He has chosen us in Him before the world's foundation, that we should be holy and blameless before Him in love." In 1 Peter 1:20 the Scripture says that God redeemed you with the precious blood of the Lord Jesus before the foundation of the world. It makes a very clear point that you were not redeemed with things like silver and gold, but with the most precious commodity in the universe — the blood of the Lord Jesus Christ! The Father used the most expensive commodity in all eternity to purchase you back. He loves you that much!

Before the world began God chose you for His purpose and His grace, as it says in 1 Timothy 1:9, "He has saved us and called us to a holy life—not because of anything we have done, but because of His own purpose and grace. This grace was given to us in Christ Jesus before the beginning of time." This passage makes it clear that it had nothing to do with anything that you have done but everything to do with His perfect purpose and grace. Before the foundations of the world, before time began, before the universe existed, God chose to redeem you to Himself and give your life meaning and purpose. The method He chose to accomplish this extraordinary plan, was one of the most brutal human instruments of death — the cross. Why the cross, you ask? The cross was a brutal Roman instrument of death. God took an instrument of man designed for death and made it an instrument of God to bring life!

The law fully fulfilled on our behalf

Jesus lived a perfect life so that all the requirements of the law would be fully fulfilled in Him. He said that He did not come to abolish the law but to fulfill it.

He spent a great deal of His ministry on Earth resetting the high standards of the law. The Pharisees and teachers of the law had reduced the law to achievable human standards. Many times He used the phrase, "you have heard it said... but I tell you." He raised the standard of the law back to its perfect place and demanded that everyone be perfect even as the heavenly Father is perfect (Matthew 5:48). They talked about adultery, but Jesus said if they even looked at a woman lustfully they had committed adultery with her. They reduced the standards and Jesus put them above human attainment — on purpose. He wanted them (and us) to get it — we cannot do this. We will always be law-breakers. Our self righteousness will never work. We need a Savior!

Once it was clear to everyone that there was no option to lower the standards of the law to fit their tradition — to make it humanly possible - Jesus told them that He himself was the only solution for mankind. He said that He was the bread of life and whoever ate of that bread would have eternal life. He said that whoever came to Him and drank would never be thirsty again. Again and again He showed that He alone was the only person ever to walk planet Earth that would be able to perfectly fulfill the law and all its requirements. The law can never make us righteous — it can only show us up and point to our need for a Savior.

He made it abundantly clear that even if you break one element of the law you are a lawbreaker and are therefore guilty of it all. With such impossible standards He wanted us to finally admit that we are not capable of living perfect lives through our own strength and effort. He showed us that our self-righteousness would be as filthy rags before the Father. Our religious efforts would pale in comparison to His perfect standards.

It was not Jesus' intention to replace the old covenant laws with a bunch of new covenant laws. It was His divine intention and the purpose of His Father that He would fulfill all the law on behalf of mankind. As they nailed Him to the cross all the requirements of the law in that moment were fully fulfilled for all mankind in Jesus Christ!

The sin of the world laid on Jesus

When my son Luke was 10 years old, I was trying to help him understand what really happened at the cross. I decided to use a science fiction metaphor to help him visualize the idea of Jesus taking on the sin of the world into His body. I asked him to imagine that sin was like a black vapor — a murky fog-like substance of filth and destruction.

Together we pictured Jesus hanging on the cross, His body in excruciating pain with every nerve ending on fire. I said, "At this moment the Father begins the most difficult part of the plan.Pretend that you are there and you can see sin being pulled out of all of those standing around the cross — a black vapor is sucked into the body of Jesus. The circle grows and more and more sin is pulled out of the soldiers and the spectators. The circle grows further and eventually all the sin of Jerusalem is pouring out in a thick black dark vapor into the body of Christ. As a circle expands, it moves beyond one region and slowly moves around the entire surface of the Earth — drawing out the sin of everyone who is alive — into His body. As He held that sin, the physical pain now pails in comparison, overshadowed by the pain of the sin of the whole world on Him.

The Father whispers, "Have you got it Son?" And the Son, in His spirit, replies, "I've got it Father". Then the Father rolls back time to the beginning of mankind and all the sin of all the people that lived before, is drawn out and the vapor is incredibly thick and the sin so heavy. It was all drawn into the broken body of Jesus. With all the sins of those past and those present, the Father winds time forward to the end of our age and draws out all the sin of all mankind from the future, into the precious body of His Son.

At that moment the Father turns His face away from His only Son so that one day He would never have to turn His face away from you. And then, with all the sin of the world past, present and future, Jesus gives up His life willingly. It showed the world that the sacrifice was greater than the sin! The perfect lamb was slain for all mankind."

What were you planning to add to that? What good deed or self righteous effort could add to the perfect work of the cross on your behalf?

"And by that will, we have been made holy through the sacrifice of the body of Jesus Christ once for all" (Hebrews 10:10). "The death he died, he died to sin once for all; but the life he lives, he lives to God" (Romans 6:10).

It was not the sacrifice of the law of goats and calves, but the perfect sacrifice of the perfect Lamb of God that once and for all reunited us with the Father. As the Bible says in Hebrews 9:12, "He did not enter by means of the blood of goats and calves; but he entered the Most Holy Place once for all by his own blood, thus obtaining eternal redemption."

The great exchange

You are of such great value that the Father used the most expensive commodity in the universe to purchase you back from sin and death. He paid with the precious blood of His Son - Jesus. Now you are not your own, you are bought with a price. (1 Corinthians 6:19-20).

A great exchange took place that day: All that was due to you was put on Jesus and all that was due to Jesus was put on you. What an extraordinary exchange! All sin, all sickness and disease, all curses, all failure and poverty, all defeats and faithlessness — all that was on your life was taken off you and put on Jesus.

All the Father's love, His righteousness and holiness, His healing and purity, His blessing and favor, all that was on His life was put on you! The day you believed on the Lord Jesus Christ you activated that great exchange in your life. The greatest miracle of all creation took place: you moved from death to life, from a sinner to a saint, from one cursed to one blessed, from an object of wrath to a beloved son or daughter. Praise God!

The effects are permanent

Once the great exchange has taken place, the effects are permanent. In the following chapters we are going to explore the details of this great exchange.

You have been given an extraordinary gift — the gift of righteousness. It is not your behavior that puts you in right standing with God the Father, but Jesus' perfect behavior on your behalf. Now it is up to you to live a life worthy of that great sacrifice and that is a whole lot easier than you can possibly imagine.

You no longer have to earn that which Jesus has freely given you. The effects of the cross are permanent: you have been permanently set free from sin, the law, and worldliness. These three things were nailed to the cross when Jesus died for you. Jesus has broken the power of sin and death over your life once and for all as confirmed in Romans 8:2, "Because through Christ Jesus the law of the Spirit who gives life has set you free from the law of sin and death."

All the requirements of the law have been fully fulfilled in you in Jesus. Look at Romans 8:4, "In order that the righteous requirement of **the**

law might be fully met in us, who do not live according to the flesh but according to the Spirit." Therefore, you do not have to live according to the flesh but according to the Spirit. The precious Holy Spirit is now the means by which you live and the power by which you walk in all that Jesus has paid for you to enjoy. In the chapters that follow, we will explore how easy that is to do. Remember, Jesus encouraged us by declaring that His yoke is easy and His burden is light.

Just like Adam and Eve, you have a choice to keep what God has given you or to believe a lie and give it away. Jesus has given you His righteousness and set you free. In this extraordinary position all you have to do is keep it. You do not have to mimic it, imitate it, invent it, make your own version of it, or develop your own self-righteousness. You are free from it all.

Galatians 5:1 says, "It is for freedom that Christ has set us free. Stand firm, then, <u>and do not *let*</u> yourselves be burdened again by a yoke of slavery."

There is that "let" word again. Once again you have been given authority to let yourself stay free in Christ. Keep your freedom. Stay in the place Jesus earned on your behalf. Don't give it up for a lie. The enemy will challenge you using the same old strategies he has always used: "Did God really say?" He will challenge your identity in Christ. He used this on Jesus in the desert, "If you are the son of God, then...." The enemy has not had an original idea since he left Heaven.

The most successful strategy the enemy has deployed against the church is getting her to think that she can earn what Jesus has already freely given her. Somehow he has convinced us that Jesus only went part of the way and it is our job to finish it. As if in some way, through our human effort, behavior modification and our self-righteousness can add to the perfect work of the cross. That somehow we can complete the master plan that God the Father, God the Son, and God the Holy Spirit put into effect before the foundations of the world. How absurd for us to believe that.

There is nothing you can add to the perfect work of the cross. Once Jesus sets you free you are free indeed. Jesus said so himself, "So if the Son sets you free, you will be free indeed" in John 8:36.

Enjoy your freedom in Christ.

10

CHAPTER TEN

YOUR IDENTITY IN CHRIST

Let's take a moment to recap what we have learned so far. We have seen that our inner being is called the *soul* and that at the center of the *soul* we have the *heart*. We learned that the *heart* consists of the mind, will, emotions, and conscience. At the center of the *heart* is the *spirit* — our human spirit. When we became believers our *spirit* was made alive to God and became the fountain of life within. We've taken time to see how the *spirit* can inform our minds, ignite our emotions, direct our will, and regulate our conscience. The diagram shows life flowing from our *spirit* into our *heart*.

Your true identity - sense of self

In an earlier chapter we learned that the soul is our sense of our true self — the "I". Now we can complete our model by looking at this last outer ring called the soul. As the life of God flows into our hearts, our hearts overflow to inform us of who we are. "For as he thinketh in his soul [nephesh], so is he" (Proverbs 23:7a DBY).

If I have worldly thinking, my soul — my sense of self — is incorrectly informed. If I allow myself to be defined by the world — by worldly thinking — then I become the sum total of my past, my successes and failures, my education, my ethnicity, my gender, my cultural upbringing, my job, and my bank balance.

Spiritual thinking defines me differently.

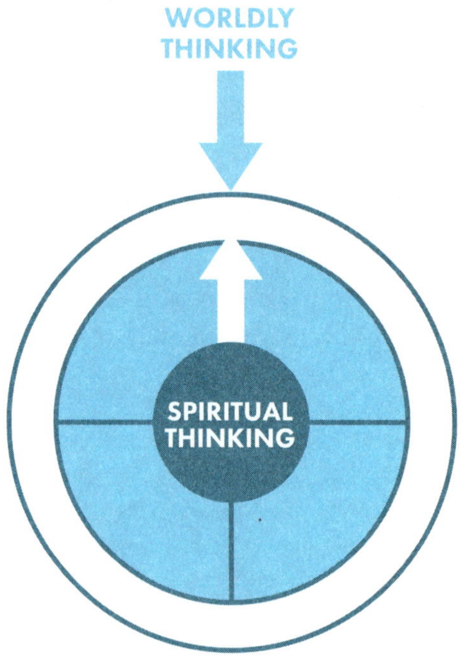

I am a beloved son of the King. I was a sinner but now I am a saint by His free gift. I am the righteousness of God in Christ and I can do all things through Christ who strengthens me.

The battle of definition

This is the direct conflict that happens in the realm of the *soul*: I can allow the life of God to overflow from my *heart* and define me, or I can allow the world to define me.

The interesting thing about how the world defines you is how very fickle it is and how it can change quickly for better or for worse. Have you ever noticed how you are perceived differently by different groups? At work you may be perceived one way, at church you are perceived another way, and at the neighborhood cookout you're perceived differently too. All these perceptions are based on a small sample of what flows out of your *heart* and manifests in your behavior and attitudes. People are forming opinions about you based off very little information — for the most part. So the definitions that people offer are not based on a deep knowledge of your *heart*. People will constantly offer you their view of who they think you are.

Sticky note definitions

My friend (and the senior pastor of our church), Greg Haswell, uses the analogy of sticky notes being stuck on you as you meet people. Imagine every time you meet somebody, their view is stuck on you like a sticky note. So on your outside, there are all sorts of sticky notes that others have stuck on in their attempt to understand you and interact with you. Perhaps some of the notes may read: *smart, arrogant, humble, quiet, weak, fun, boring, uninteresting, fascinating*, etc. But none of these sticky notes are the real you. They may be accurate in some aspects and be completely wrong in others. What's worse, is that many of the sticky notes would contradict each other depending on context. People at church may find you boring while people at work see you as fascinating. People's sticky note definitions are created on-the-fly. They do not spend hours contemplating or thinking about it. The sticky note definitions happen automatically as part of normal human interactions. In and of themselves, they are not dangerous until we believe them. It is critical that you do not develop worldly thinking and allow the sticky notes to define who you are.

On occasion, some sticky notes will be aligned with who you truly are in your heart. In a later chapter we're going to talk about how to see people as God sees them. If you're blessed to have people in your life who take this view of you, you may have many more sticky notes aligned with your heart than most people would have.

Who you are in your heart is the real you. You cannot respond to a collection of sticky notes or define your life by them. There is a deep definition from Heaven that you need to understand. We saw in an earlier Scripture when we're talking about David that said man looks at the outer appearance but God looks at the heart.

God sees you differently

There is a great story in the Bible about a man named Gideon. Israel was being oppressed by the Midianites. This had been going on for seven years and Israel was suffering under their brutal invasion. Everything Israel grew — crops and livestock — the Midianites consumed. It was so bad that they were hiding in shelters in the mountains to get away from their oppressors. They called out to God and in response He sent an angel. Now this part is really fascinating. The angel did not go to the leader of Israel but to a young man named Gideon who was hiding in a wine press trying to press wheat there.

Let's pick up the story in Judges 6: 12-15: "When the angel of the LORD appeared to Gideon, he said, 'The LORD is with you, mighty warrior.' 'Pardon me, my lord,' Gideon replied, 'but if the LORD is with us, why has all this happened to us? Where are all his wonders that our ancestors told us about when they said, 'Did not the LORD bring us up out of Egypt?' But now the LORD has abandoned us and given us into the hand of Midian.' The LORD turned to him and said, 'Go in the strength you have and save Israel out of Midian's hand. Am I not sending you?' 'Pardon me, my lord,' Gideon replied, 'but how can I save Israel? My clan is the weakest in Manasseh, and I am the least in my family.'"

I love this story because it shows that God defines us differently. When the Lord appeared to Gideon He said to him, "The Lord is with you, mighty warrior." Remember that Gideon was not acting like a mighty warrior in any fashion or form. In fact, he was hiding and acting very much like he was intimidated by the enemy. His outward behavior would define him as a coward and a wimp. But God looked at his heart and called him by his real name "mighty warrior."

Immediately, Gideon resists God's definition and pointed to outward events to contradict what God had just said to him. He said to God, "If you're with us why is all this bad stuff happening?" In Gideon's mind he disagreed with both parts of what God said: that God was with them and that he was a mighty warrior. But if you look closely, God did not say He was with Israel - He said He was with Gideon.

In Heaven, Gideon was known by his real name "mighty warrior." Before Gideon had performed any acts of valor, he was a mighty warrior in his heart. His acts of valor would prove to others what he already was in his heart. Gideon continues to argue with God saying that he was not qualified to be God's mighty warrior claiming, "My clan is the weakest in Manasseh, and I am the least in my family." Gideon's mechanism for defining himself was based on external, outward and worldly thinking. Based on that criteria he did not qualify to do anything great for God. After all, he came from a weak clan and within that clan he was the least. But God saw him differently. He said, "If you will believe my definition of you, and believe that I am with you, I will use my strength to help you deliver the nation from the enemy."

What heaven sees

People see you one way, but God sees you as you are known in Heaven. Who does Heaven say you are? Who is the real you? What has God built into your inner being? Do you know? And if you did know would you believe it? These are the core issues that drive our identity in Christ.

Imagine the day that you arrive in Heaven and you're being introduced to the Angels and all the saints. What name will they call you? You know what Gideon would have said and he was wrong. You know how others in Heaven knew him long before he did anything to earn that name: *mighty warrior.*

The problem with many believers today is their worldly thinking that defines who they think they are. But there is wonderful news! You do not have to live another day under the wrong definition that others have placed on you or that you have placed on yourself. You can drop of the collection of sticky notes, and ask God to reveal to you who you truly are. It may take a little time but God is very eager to share with you how He sees you and how you are known to Him.

A few months ago, my wife Bridget and my daughter Lindsay ran a small group called "Discovering your identity in Christ". Over the 10 weeks that they met, people's lives were transformed as they began to discover their true identity in Christ. On the very first night Bridget talked about the Gideon story and she invited each of them to find a quiet place in the church and to ask God to show them how He saw them. It was astounding to hear that in less than one hour, people's perception of themselves began to dramatically change as the Lord revealed to them who they truly are.

Perhaps this type of exercise sounds frightening. Perhaps you are afraid that your own imagination would dominate the process. Allow me to encourage you to trust the Lord. If any of your children came to you and asked you a sincere question, would you sit in silence and leave them guessing? I think not. How much more will your heavenly Father desire to answer such an important question?

How you feel about yourself

We have talked a lot about what you think about yourself but we can apply the same mechanism to every area of the *heart*. We've made a strong case for the fact that your soul definition needs to come out of the overflow of your *heart* — the definition from God.

This applies to what you feel about yourself too. When we think wrongly about ourselves it generates wrong emotions and negativity. Neuroscience has discovered that toxic thoughts drive chemical changes in our bodies — into every cell in the human body. Toxicity in our body can often be traced to toxic thoughts. Negative emotions about ourselves are often driven by a poor view of who we think we are. That is why it is so critical that you know what God thinks of you. This will release joyful and peaceful emotions in you and your physical body will feel the difference.

Some neuroscience research indicates that believing positive things releases powerful healing chemistry in your body which ties in beautifully with Proverbs 14:30, "A heart at peace gives life to the body, but envy rots the bones." Positive thoughts and beliefs rewire the brain and some research suggests that the brain can be rewired in less than a week.

It is great when science confirms what the Scripture says, but that does not change the fact that God has put powerful weapons in your hands. It is critical that you take every negative thought captive and make it submit to the truth. Remember the verse about powerful weapons?

"We demolish arguments and every pretension that sets itself up against the knowledge of God, and we take captive every thought to make it obedient to Christ" (2 Corinthians 10:5 NIV).

When you take thoughts captive, you create alignment with Heaven and you release the fountain of life in your inner being. Everything changes. Even your body feels the effects of these new life-giving thoughts.

Some of the thoughts that need to be taken captive involve what we believe about God, who He is, and who we are in Him. Before we can build a powerful identity in Christ we need to understand the power of Christ in us. The revelation of who Christ is in us will define who we think we are in Him.

So we've come to that point in the book, where we have to create alignment with Heaven in who Christ is in us. This means settling some key issues in our hearts so that our thoughts can release the fountain of life in us and to those around us.

After several decades of ministry, I have come to see that many believers in the body of Christ are struggling with their relationship with God. They do not believe that they are truly forgiven or that they deserve to be forgiven because of the things they have done, thought, or said.

Some of us may be clear about the wonderful news of the new covenant and the gospel of grace, but others may be still trying to live a mixture of the old covenant and the new covenant which causes devastating results. The apostle Paul said that if we submit ourselves again to the old covenant law, we nullify the cross and that this mixture is no gospel at all.

We will now step out to explore the good news of Jesus Christ. As we do this, you'll discover the wonderful freedom that Jesus purchased on your behalf. Your relationship with God will break through into new heights as you realize what He has done for you.

I ask that you will temporarily suspend what you may have been previously taught and take a fresh look at what the Scriptures presents for itself. The Scripture warns us about not changing the truth for the sake of our traditions.

Often when life does not line up with what we believe we're tempted to change what we believe. There is a better alternative: to become clear about what the Bible teaches, and expect life to submit to the truth of God's word. We will avoid the temptation to change our theology to fit our experience but rather expect that our experiences will be aligned with the wonderful truth of the new covenant in Jesus.

In the following chapters you will learn:

- You are forgiven!
- You are dead to sin!
- You have a new nature!
- You are one with Christ!

Let's get started...

CHAPTER ELEVEN

YOU ARE TRULY FORGIVEN

For you to establish your true identity in Christ, there are several things that you need to settle once and for all in your own heart. Once you settle these things in your inner man it will be much easier for you to think differently about yourself. Your identity in Christ is based on this mechanism: you need to be clear about who Christ is in you before you can be clear about who you are in Him.

In the next few chapters we need to cover several key Scriptures to settle these issues. Now, if you are like most people, you may be tempted to skip through the Scriptures and to read past them. Please do not do that! I am making a special request to you that you carefully read the Scriptures so that you can see for yourself what the Bible teaches. It is so important that you do not rely purely on the interpretation of others or on your church background. You must see it for yourself for you to believe it in your heart. Once the truth takes hold in your inner being you will be transformed.

Learning to repent

The Scripture says that we are transformed by the renewing of our minds. Look at Romans 12:2, "Do not conform to the pattern of this world, but be transformed by the renewing of your mind. Then you will be able to test and approve what God's will is--his good, pleasing and perfect will." It is also important to understand that when in the New Testament uses the word repent, it means "to change your mind" or "to take a new mind" on the matter.

The word in Greek is *metanoia*. Wikipedia summarizes the work of Edward J. Anton in *Repentance: A Cosmic Shift of Mind and Heart,* as follows: "Anton observes that in the minds of most Christians the primary meaning of 'repent' is to look back on past behavior with sorrow, self-reproach, or contrition, sometimes with an amendment of life. But neither Jesus nor John the Baptist says to look back in sorrow. For St Paul, 'metanoia is a transfiguration for your brain' that opens a new future."

This is why so many great theologians feel that the translation of the word *metanoia* as "repent" in English, is the greatest mistranslation in the New Testament. Our English word "repent" has us always looking back and trying to ask God for forgiveness in an attempt to be in right standing with Him. But this is not the gospel that Paul taught. The gospel is forward-looking. Jesus wants you to be living in the present and looking to the future that He has for you. He asked you to believe Him and to believe who you are in Him. For this to be possible, He's forgiven all your sins: past, present and future — once and for all. When you believe that you are truly forgiven, your mind changes dramatically. The way you pray, the way you live, and the way you worship changes permanently.

You must therefore be clear in your heart of who you are in Christ so that your mind can be renewed. Transformation is effortless. Your new thinking is based on what you know in your spirit to be true. So the key then is to be certain about what you believe Jesus did for you at the cross. This clarity in your heart will inform your mind.

To help you with this process we need to settle several elements of the new covenant. As you settle each of these in your heart your life will be transformed. Let's take a look at each of these.

I am always forgiven

One of the hardest things for Christians to believe is that they are truly forgiven. The reason for this is that we have mixed two covenants in our general preaching. We have blended elements of the old covenant with elements of the new covenant. It is really important that we divide the two. Jesus fulfilled all the requirements of the old covenant and through His death and resurrection introduced the new covenant. Under the old covenant, your blessing and forgiveness was based on your own performance. Under the new covenant however, your forgiveness and blessing is based on the perfect performance of Jesus on your behalf.

Let's take a look at 1 John 1:9, "If we confess our sins, He is faithful and righteous to forgive us our sins and to cleanse us from all unrighteousness." This is a very important verse because it tells us much more than we get from reading the English only. In Greek there are different tenses and these give us more information than we get from our limited tenses in English. For instance, the words "forgive" and "cleanse" in the Greek are in a special tense which tells us that these are a one time event — never to be repeated.

The word "confess" is in a different tense which tells us that it is a continual process. So what does this all mean? It means that when we come to Christ we were forgiven and cleansed as a one-time event. The Scripture allows freedom to confess as many times as we like —

continually if we wish. The subsequent confessions do not make us anymore forgiven because forgiveness happened once for all — a one-time event.

When you came to Jesus and gave your life to Him, you simply prayed something like: "I confess that I'm a sinner and I believe in you Jesus, please forgive me, cleanse me and come into my life". You did not take a sheet of paper and try to list every sin that you'd committed in your life to that point. Even if you attempted that, we can with great certainty declare that you would have missed many of them. All the sins you have committed: intentional sin, unintentional sin, things you did that were not in faith (the Bible says anything not done in faith is sin) and the sins of omission — stuff you didn't do but should've done. All these sins would be impossible to list. It is safe to say that it is impossible to confess all your sins on the day you came to Christ.

What you did, the day you became a believer, was confess that Christ was sufficient and accept His death on the cross on your behalf. Why is it then that we believe from that day on we have to keep confessing our sins to maintain our forgiveness? If it is now up to us to remember if we sin (including those that we are unaware of and those sins committed by our lack of obedience or lack of faith) then no one person on this Earth is in right standing with God. What we are really saying is that if it is up to us to keep confessing our sins to stay right with God, then there is no salvation in Christ. It is an impossible task. Why would God go to such extraordinary lengths to deal with your sin once for all only to leave it to your memory to keep you in right standing with Him? God's forgiveness is bigger than that.

But the good news of the gospel is that when you came to Christ you were forgiven once for all. Think about it: how many of your sins were in the future when Jesus died for you? Yes, they were all in the future — every one of them. The day you became a believer and accepted Jesus Christ as your Lord and Savior, you accepted that all your sins were forgiven but all those sins were in the future the day Jesus died. So the Scripture gives us a wonderful option: come to Jesus, confess that you are a sinner in need of a Savior, and He will forgive and cleanse you once for all — with no need to repeat that process again.

Confession in the new covenant is different than the old covenant

If confession of sin was the primary method of staying right with God then surely the apostle Paul would have mentioned it at least once? Paul never used this phrase "confession of sin" but he used the phrase "make Christ your confession". Here we see another important distinction between the old covenant and the new covenant. In the old covenant, people are sin conscious and need to bring constant sacrifices for their sin - at least once a year. Those sacrifices lasted for one year and then needed to be continually repeated to stay in right standing with God.

But under the new covenant it is an entirely different method. The perfect Lamb was sacrificed once for all. His blood is so powerful that no other sacrifices are needed. The new covenant teaches that when we come to Christ, He forgives us our sin and cleanses us from all unrighteousness — once for all — with no need for continual repetition. Now that is good news!

If we try to mix the new and the old covenants together and teach that we need to confess our sins to stay in right standing with God, then we're saying that the blood of bulls and goats is more powerful than the blood of Jesus. At least the sacrifices of bulls and goats lasted the whole year. Many of us have been taught that we are only as good as our last confession. This is simply not the teaching of the gospel of Christ. It is not the new covenant that Jesus instituted. Remember, remember, remember the new covenant is far more wonderful than that. The blood of bulls and goats only <u>*covered*</u> your sins but under the new covenant the blood of Jesus Christ <u>*cleanses*</u> you from all unrighteousness. Wow!

The role of confession for the new covenant believer

So, is it wrong for believers to confess their sins? Not at all. Remember that the word "confess" in 1 John 1:9 is something that we can continually do. We are in a relationship with the Lord and if we have done something that is wrong it is only natural that we apologize — as one would do in any relationship. But this apology does not make us anymore forgiven. We are free to confess our sins as much as we would like to but it is important that we understand that we are already forgiven and cleansed from all unrighteousness. Confession does not lead to forgiveness, Jesus' blood does.

James 5:16 says, "Therefore confess your sins to each other and pray for each other so that you may be healed." Some people have a difficult time believing they are forgiven and when they confess their sins to someone else, they find a release and their forgiveness becomes real to them. They are healed. The forgiveness was already purchased for them but a friend or counsellor helped them make that a reality in their lives. This a great application for confession of sin in a new covenant context which James says will help us find healing for our souls and our bodies.

Christ conscious versus sin conscious

The Lord wants you to be Christ conscious under the new covenant and not sin conscious like those under the old covenant. We cannot drive forward while watching the rearview mirror. The Lord want us looking forward and not backward. He wants us to see our future in Christ and not the sin of our past. He paid a dear price for that sin, so accept His total forgiveness and begin living in the wonder of your new righteousness in Christ Jesus.

God wants you to understand that you have a wonderful future in Him and that there is now no need for you to sin, be worldly, or be bound by the law. You are free in Jesus to serve Him and to enjoy your destiny in God. You are free from the law, free from sin and free from worldliness.

Is this a license to sin?

Some may read this and think that I am teaching people to sin or giving them a license to sin. Not at all! Let me ask you this: if you were $500,000 in debt and I wrote a check for the full amount, gave it to you and in addition I put an additional $20 million into your bank account for all your future needs, what is your first thought? Would it not be completely insane for you to think, "Great now I can go back into debt." Anyone who has been forgiven all their sins — and who understands this — their first thought is not how to go back into sin but how to please the Lord and live a life worthy of His sacrifice.

He who is forgiven much loves much

In Luke 7:41-47, Jesus told the story about a moneylender who had loaned money to two people. To the one he had lent 500 denarii and to the other 50 denarii. Neither could repay their debt and so the moneylender forgave them both. Jesus asked which one would love the moneylender more. Simon replied, "I suppose the one who had the bigger debt forgiven." Jesus said to him, "You have judged correctly." The reason Jesus told the story is that He was in a Pharisee's house when a woman who had lived a sinful life came into the house and washed His feet with her tears and wiped them with her hair, and lovingly poured perfume on them. The Pharisee thought to himself, "If this man were a prophet, he would know who is touching him and what kind of woman she is — that she's a sinner". Jesus went on to say, "Therefore, I tell you, her many sins have been forgiven — as her great love has shown. But whoever has been forgiven little loves little."

Jesus made it clear: if you believe that you are a pretty good person and that there is not much wrong with you — that you are really about 90% there — and all you need from God is the last bit to make you great, **then you will love little.** If you believe you are forgiven little, you will love little. If you believe you are forgiven much, you will love much.

The truth about the gospel of grace is that every one of us has been forgiven millions of denarii and therefore we love much. Any thought that we were forgiven little is based in an evil deception of the heart. There is not one among us who is righteous — no not one. We all <u>were</u> sinners saved by grace and <u>now</u> we are saints. By the free gift of God's grace and His great mercy towards us, every one of us has been forgiven way more than we even understand. Our first thought, now that we are completely forgiven, is not how we can go back to sin, but how we can keep the righteousness Jesus so freely gave us.

Think of it this way. Under the law, if you break one law you are a law breaker and guilty of breaking all the law. Since the law is perfect and cannot bend or its standards be lowered, that means we are all law breakers. So, when we came to Christ, He forgave us for being law breakers. We are all forgiven the same amount — being guilty of breaking all the law. Wow! What a great forgiveness.

I am dead to sin

If you thought being forgiven completely is good news, hang onto your hat, it gets better. The Bible teaches us that under the new covenant, not only are our sins forgiven, but God has broken the power of sin and death over us. The living Bible translation puts it beautifully in Romans 6:10, "When he died, he died once to break the power of sin. But now that he lives, he lives for the glory of God."

This means that once you lived in a prison called sin and in that place you committed many sins. It was your nature to do so. Not only did Jesus wipe clean the record of all your sins, but He broke you out of the prison of sin and set you free. Look at this verse in Romans 6:11, "In the same way, count yourselves dead to sin but alive to God in Christ Jesus." Now you're alive to God - permanently free from the power of sin in your life. From God's point of view, there is no need that you should ever sin again. How free is that? Sin no longer has any hold on you. Once you believe this in your heart, your thinking will change and your life will be transformed. Say to yourself, "I am a saint made holy and righteous as a free gift from Jesus. Sin has no power over me. I'm dead to sin and alive to God"

Why do I still sin?

As Graham Cooke, the international speaker and author, so eloquently says, "The best way to be dead to sin is to be alive to God." You may ask, "If I'm dead to sin and made holy and righteous, why do I still sin?" "Is it possible for believers to sin?" Let's look at this verse in 1 John 3:9, "No one who is born of God will continue to sin, because God's seed remains in them; they cannot go on sinning, because they have been born of God." Here John tells us that righteous people do righteous things. Once you realize the truth that you are indeed dead to sin, and that sin has no power over you, your mind becomes renewed. You change your mind (*metanoia*) about who you are and who God is in you.

Let me illustrate this with a story. A man in our church had been addicted to pornography since his early teenage years. Now in his 50s, he spent more than 40 years living under condemnation. He tried every program he could find. He been for counseling and enrolled in various programs, but did not break free. When he read verses like Romans 8:1,

"There is now therefore no condemnation to them who are in Christ Jesus," he simply did not believe it.

When he heard the teaching of the new covenant — that he is completely forgiven and that he is now the righteousness of God in Christ - he realized the great disconnect between what the new covenant teaches and where he lives. As we talked, I told him that it was important that he believed the truth in his heart that he is the righteousness of God in Christ and that sin has no power over him. He looked at me with a disbelief in his eyes and said, "Are you telling me that when I sit in front of my computer on these porn sites that I am the righteousness of God in Christ? Are you saying that before, during and after that sin I am still the righteousness of God in Christ?" I responded, "Absolutely! Jesus' gift to you was unconditional as is His love for you."

We started a simple process of daily confession of Christ. Every day he had to declare, "I am the righteousness of God in Christ according to 2 Corinthians 5:21. I am dead to sin and alive to God according to Romans 6:11." I encouraged him to make this confession as many times a day as he felt necessary. I told him there will come a day that he will believe the truth in his heart and that this truth would renew his mind and transform his life. I received a call six months later, and this is what he said, "I just had to call you and tell you that for the first time in my life I am free!" I could hear the tears of joy in his voice, and he explained, "I started making those confessions that you gave me and went on to add others from the Scriptures. It did not stop immediately — it kind of gradually faded away. One day an incredible realization hit me: I have not watched any porn in six weeks! It just happened automatically. I wasn't trying to give it up. I simply believed who Jesus says I am in Him. You know, I really am the righteousness of God in Christ! Wow!"

This is a wonderful example of effortless change that happens when we believe. You may ask why it took so long. The answer is that it took this man many months to believe who he is in Christ. <u>The length of the process is only limited by the time it takes us to believe.</u>

The Bible teaches that when Christ died, you died with Him and when He rose from the dead you rose with Him. Look at these verses: Romans 6:8, "Now if we died with Christ, we believe that we will also live with him" Col 2:20, "Since you died with Christ to the elemental spiritual forces of this world, why, as though you still belonged to the world, do you submit to its rules". Finally, Col 3:3 "For you died, and your life is now hidden with Christ in God."

The bottom line is that your old life is dead. You died with Christ, were buried, and raised in newness of life with Him.

Acts 13:38-39 says, "Therefore, my friends, I want you to know that through Jesus the forgiveness of sins is proclaimed to you. Through him **everyone who believes is set free from every sin**, a justification you were not able to obtain under the law of Moses."

It is time for us to believe and be free from every sin.

12

CHAPTER TWELVE

YOUR GIFT OF RIGHTEOUSNESS

If you have accepted that you are forgiven and free from sin, it is now time to settle a third issue in your heart. This is the issue of what makes you righteous. In this section I'm going to use a lot of Scripture because it's vital that this issue is settled from a biblical viewpoint. There has been much debate and confusion in the church as to the role of the law as it applies to new covenant believers. We're going to see that the righteousness that comes by faith is a free gift from the Lord. The law cannot make you righteous.

Righteous deeds cannot make you righteous. Only the blood of Christ can do that by faith.

Moreover, if we put ourselves back under the law we commit ourselves to a system of self-righteousness and nullify the effects of the cross. These are very bold statements, so we need to take a careful walk through each aspect to ensure that this is truly what the Bible teaches.

Why is the subject of righteousness so important? Why is it not acceptable to God that we do our best? Why has He set the standard so impossibly high?

The Father has set His love upon us. He desires to restore us to the original glory He intended for us. This is only possible in the atmosphere of holiness and righteousness. Sin is a dramatic constrictor of life. Sin is like a python that gets its hook in you and slowly squeezes the life out of you. The enemy and the world would like us to believe that living a life of sin is true freedom. Nothing could be further from the truth! Sin demands more and more and gives less and less. It is the very nature of evil. But God is good and in His goodness He gives everything for nothing. He asks that we believe in His son Jesus Christ.

When the Father set up the old covenant, He made it clear that if those under that covenant were careful to do everything that the law commanded them, then they would be blessed in everything that they do. Their crops would be blessed, their children would be blessed, their work would be blessed and all aspects of life would flourish under the blessing of the Lord. But, on the other hand, if they did not perfectly obey the law, they set themselves up to be cursed.

Who is first?

Under the old covenant, the formula was: **First you then God**. First you behaved then God would bless you. First you forgave others and then God would forgive you. If you did not forgiven others you were not forgiven.

Under the new covenant, the formula is: **First God then you.** Because God has freely forgiven you, so you must freely forgive others. First God gave you the gift of righteousness now you walk in it.

Righteousness is the basis of blessing and God's favor. Jesus came and fulfilled all the requirements of the law on your behalf so that all the promises and all the blessing can be yours. You can read through the old covenant and claim all the benefits of its promises because of

Jesus. Isn't that wonderful? Now you read the Old Testament with very different eyes, don't you?

Paul taught this in 2 Corinthians 1:20, "For no matter how many promises God has made, they are 'Yes' in Christ. And so through him the 'Amen' is spoken by us to the glory of God." Wow! All God's promises made throughout the Scriptures have become "yes" to us in Christ and it is our job to simply say "so be it" (which is what the word amen means). So let's take a closer look at how the Bible views righteousness.

I am the righteousness of God in Christ

There are only two kinds of righteousness in the Scriptures: self-righteousness and the gift of righteousness. Paul said in Galatians 2:21, "I do not nullify the grace of God; for if righteousness comes through the Law, then Christ died needlessly." In several places Paul made it clear that a person is justified by faith alone apart from the works of the law. The law cannot make anyone righteous it can only show them the standard that they are falling short of. By its very structure, the law shows our deficiency and condemns us for the shortfall. It has been designed by the Father to be the great school master and show us our need for a Savior. Gal. 3:24, "Therefore the Law has become our tutor to lead us to Christ, that we may be justified by faith."

Paul says in Romans 3:28, "For we maintain that a man is justified by faith apart from works of the Law." It is by grace and grace alone that we are saved and made righteous. I love the way Paul puts it in Romans 11:6, "But if it is by grace, it is no longer on the basis of works, otherwise grace is no longer grace." If your works are the basis of your righteousness then grace is no longer grace and in fact there is no need for grace because you are depending on your own self-righteousness. But praise God there is no need for that. Jesus has made a way and has given you the free gift of righteousness.

You are the righteousness of God in Christ according to 2 Corinthians 5:21, "God made him who had no sin to be sin for us, so that in him we might become the righteousness of God."

Paul goes even further to say that if righteousness was based on our own works then it would not be a gift but in fact an obligation from God that He would owe us. In the same way that if somebody worked a job, the salary at the end of the month is not a gift but an obligation that must be paid to them because it's based on their performance and their hard work. But this righteousness that we have is a righteousness given to us as a free gift. Our self-righteousness is as filthy rags before the Lord and cannot attain the full requirements of the law. Look at Romans 4:4-5, "Now to the one who works, wages are not credited as a gift but as an obligation. However, to the one who does not work but trusts God who justifies the ungodly, their faith is credited as righteousness."

By now I'm sure you are getting the point. If you choose the path of self-righteousness you commit yourself to the law and you make Christ of no value. If you choose faith to receive the gift of righteousness then it is a righteousness that is based on grace and not works. These are mutually exclusive concepts. This means it is either one or the other — it cannot be both. This is exactly what Philippians 3:9 says, "And may be found in Him, <u>not having a righteousness of my own derived from the Law,</u> but that which is through faith in Christ, the righteousness which comes from God <u>on the basis of faith.</u>"

Paul writing to the Ephesians confirms this point yet again by saying in Ephesians 2:8-9, "For by grace you have been saved through faith; and that <u>not of yourselves</u>, it is the gift of God. Not by works, lest any man should boast."

The Bible makes it clear that we have to choose one kind of righteousness or the other but we cannot mix them. Any attempt to mix self-righteousness with the gift of righteousness nullifies the cross and then Christ died needlessly.

The law no longer applies to you

In fact Paul goes on to say that for those in Christ the law has been put aside and is no longer applicable to them. Romans. 10:4, "For Christ **is the end of the law** for righteousness to everyone who believes." He says it again in Ephesians 2:14-15, "For he himself is our peace . . . by **setting aside in his flesh the law** with its commands and regulations."

So it may seem that we've really labored this point. The reason is to bring freedom in this area and deliver us from performance Christianity. I know from personal experience that if you get up on the platform and preach a performance-based message people will feel condemned and at the end of the service people will congratulate you on an excellent sermon. If on the other hand, you preach grace and you tell people that they are delivered from performance Christianity because Christ has performed perfectly on their behalf, there are far fewer after the service thanking you for your sermon. Why is this? I believe that much of the church has spent a great deal of time trying to earn God's approval in a sincere attempt to gain His favor. The truth however, is far more simple and considerably more wonderful. The truth is that Jesus has done it all! We now are confident in this gift of righteousness that we have so freely received by faith. When this issue settles in our hearts, our minds are freed from performance Christianity and our consciences are healed from a life of constant low grade condemnation. For truly, "there is now therefore no condemnation for those who are in Christ Jesus" (Romans 8:1).

The Father has a master plan. It was put in motion before the foundations of the world — before the universe was created God planned to reconcile man to himself. We were once lost but now we are found. We were dead <u>in</u> sin but now we are dead to sin. We once had an old nature that loved sin and suffered its brutal consequences. Now we have a new nature in Christ and by His free gift we have been made perfectly righteous and holy. It is by faith from first to last.

A few years ago I was preaching in our church and I wanted to drive home this point about righteousness not being based on our own effort but being based on faith and faith alone. So without warning, in the middle of my sermon I asked, "Will all the perfectly righteous people in the auditorium please stand." And I waited. The reaction of the congregation was very interesting. We have been teaching this concept for years but still people hesitated to stand. It seemed that their hesitation was based on making a public declaration of their own self-righteousness. As though they were saying, "Hey I'm perfect look at me." The point of the sermon was exactly the opposite. None of us in and of ourselves can ever achieve the righteousness that has been so freely given to us. I asked the question because I wanted to see if the people truly believed it. After some awkwardness, I asked the congregation to be seated and I explained again that we are made righteous in Jesus by a free gift and it's not our own works. I asked one more time for all the perfectly righteous people in the auditorium to stand and this time the response was spectacular. All stood! Now that's progress in our new covenant thinking.

If we do not believe in our hearts that we are holy and righteous by faith, then our minds, our emotions and our will, will always lean towards sin. However, if you believe that you are the righteousness of God in Christ, your mind will be renewed to that truth and you will find your behavior changing automatically and effortlessly.

Allow me to illustrate: recently one of the rooms in our home had a serious leak and there was a huge section of the wall in the closet covered in mold. Contractors came in and tore out a good portion of the wall. The entire closet had to be rebuilt. While it was in that state of mess, it would not have bothered me at all if somebody dropped some trash in that room — it was a mess anyway. But after it had been made completely new, and somebody dropped trash in that room I would have a real issue.

In the same way if you believe that your life is still under construction then what difference does a little more sin make? Your life is in a mess anyway. But if you truly believe in your heart that God has made you a new creation and He has made all things new, then why would you want to mess that up? He has made you perfectly righteous, so stay that way.

CHAPTER THIRTEEN

YOUR NEW NATURE

The Bible teaches that you were given a new nature the day you accepted Christ. Let's take a look at this important issue we have to settle in our hearts.

I have a new nature

Carl grew up in Tennessee and did not have much. He was careful with money and studied hard to become a pharmacist. He and two business partners spent years building their pharmaceutical company in Atlanta. The day came when a private equity firm from New York purchased the company. That is the day that every business owner and entrepreneur dreams about — the day you sell the business and all the effort and sacrifice makes it worth it. Carl and his wife built a beautiful home to reflect the change of status. They chose a new lifestyle to fit their new status. Carl and his wife are wonderful people and openly share their beautiful home. We became friends several years ago when we joined forces in a growing technology firm. Their home has been used for corporate events, school events, church events, training days, and Christmas parties. It is truly a wonderful place owned by humble people.

When you came to Christ, your status changed dramatically. You changed from a sinner to a saint. Now it is up to you to choose a lifestyle that fits your new status. In Christ you can now "afford" to live righteously and enjoy all the benefits that righteousness brings. The day you accepted Jesus as your Lord and Savior, you became a new creation. Paul writes in 2 Corinthians 5:17, "Therefore, if anyone is in Christ, the new creation has come: The old has gone, the new is here". Your old nature was crucified with Christ. You were given a new nature.

Once again we must be careful to teach the new covenant. Under this covenant, God killed your old nature and you were born again into newness of life in Jesus. No longer is it in your nature to sin. Your new nature desires to live for God, worship Him, and serve His people. The old nature previously informed your mind, will and emotions. But now you have a new nature in Christ. You have new desires, new thoughts, and new feelings. It is critical to understand that the old nature is truly dead and God does not want to talk to you about it anymore. He is interested in speaking to you about your new nature in Jesus and the extraordinary future you have in Him. He has given you a new set of desires that He has implanted in your heart. Your new nature is designed to have fellowship with God and enjoy intimacy with Him. Worship is no longer a religious duty but an expression of your new nature's ability to love Him. Giving is no longer a religious requirement but your new nature's expression of your gratitude for all the Lord has done for you. Your new nature is a direct reflection of His nature. You are now by nature generous, kind, patient, and loving.

Incredible capability of your new nature

This is why the Scriptures do not tell you to grow in patience, grow in kindness or grow in generosity. The Scripture simply says be kind, be patient, and be generous. The reason is that these instructions are natural to your new nature in Christ. These are not religious duties that you have to force yourself to do or try to emulate, but rather they are the **effortless expression of your new nature**. If your thinking is still being informed by your old nature, then you may try in your own effort to be kind, patient and generous but it will not feel authentic. Once you realize, however, that you are now a new creation and that your new nature is one with Christ and that you bear His nature, then being patient, kind and generous are easy things to do.

Keep adding Jesus' attributes to your new nature

2 Peter 1:4-9 says that we should add all the attributes that we need. This passage tells us that we increase the process of adding so that we can participate in His divine nature. It says, "Through these he has given us his very great and precious promises, so that through them you may participate in the divine nature, having escaped the corruption in the world caused by evil desires. For this very reason, make every effort to **add** to your faith goodness; and to goodness, knowledge; and to knowledge, self-control; and to self-control, perseverance; and to perseverance, godliness; and to godliness, mutual affection; and to mutual affection, love. For if you possess these qualities in increasing measure, they will keep you from being ineffective and unproductive in your knowledge of our Lord Jesus Christ. But whoever does not have them is nearsighted and blind, forgetting that they have been cleansed from their past sins."

We need to increasingly add all the attributes of Christ's nature into our lives because He has freely given them to us. We do not need to manufacture them! They are ours in Christ.

Jesus is not asking you to generate the fruits of new nature using the thinking of your old nature. This is what self-righteousness tries to do. The gift of righteousness however empowers us to do everything the Scripture asks us to do effortlessly. When the Scripture says things like be hospitable or value others more highly than yourself, it is simply explaining to you what your new nature loves to do.

If you read the Scriptures from this viewpoint, it dramatically changes the way you receive it. Instead of reading the Scriptures and feeling condemned about all the things that you're not doing, you can now read the Scriptures and get excited about all the things that your new nature is capable of doing! What a different point of view. This freedom is truly wonderful. It's like reading a will and finding all the wonderful things that you have inherited. You read page after page and it gets more and more exciting.

It's interesting that the Bible always tells you to do something because the cross enables you to do it. For example the Bible says: just as Christ has forgiven you, so forgive others. You're only asked to forgive others because you've already been forgiven and have the power to do so. The Scripture says that we ought to love one another as Christ has loved us. Once again you're only asked to do something because the power of the cross has empowered you to do it. Every command in the new covenant is based on the finished work of the cross and its power in you. Your new nature in Jesus can naturally and effortlessly do what it asks. When you read the Scriptures, do not feel that you have to invent these attributes in your own heart, but rather be thankful that Jesus has given you a new nature. Instead of thinking of *giving* as an act of obedience, think of it as an *expression* of your new nature.

Because of Jesus, you are functioning from fullness and not for fullness. You are living from God's acceptance and love and not performing for God's acceptance and love. You are not trying to earn God's favor but rather enjoying living from His favor. Do you see the distinction?

Warning: old nature thinking

When you find yourself thinking that you do not have everything you need to live a godly life, you know immediately that this is old nature thinking. New nature thinking believes what the Bible says is true. Remember in the previous chapters when we looked at the verse that said grace and peace is yours in abundance through the knowledge of God and of Jesus our Lord? His divine power has given you everything you need for a godly life through our knowledge of him who called you by His own glory and goodness (2 Peter 1: 2-4).

What counts is the new creation

This is so contrary to what many of us have been taught and yet it is the extraordinary promise of the new covenant. Everything you have in Jesus is received not earned. The kingdom is about how good you are at receiving and not how good you are at earning.

You've got to love what Paul said about the cross of Jesus in Gal 6:14-15, "May I never boast except in the cross of our Lord Jesus Christ, through which the world has been crucified to me, and I to the world. Neither circumcision nor uncircumcision means anything; what counts is the new creation." Your new nature does not connect with worldliness because the **world has been crucified to you** — it no longer has any appeal or power in your life. What counts is that you are a new creation.

When you are in the world, your freedom is in the world and the things of Christ are bothersome to you. When you are in Christ, your freedom is in Christ and the things of the world are bothersome to you.

That is why the Bible tells us to put on the new man and to put off the old. These are not lifelong processes. When the Bible says things simply it means exactly what it says. So the way to be renewed in the spirit of your mind is to put on your new man which was created according to God in true righteousness and holiness. That's exactly what Ephesians 4:23-24 says, "And be renewed in the spirit of your mind, and that you put on the new man which was created according to God, in true righteousness and holiness."

Once you've taken off your old self with all its practices and its lifestyle, put on your new self and choose a lifestyle accordingly. As you grow in your inner man in the knowledge of Jesus so you will be renewed. That is what Paul says in Col 3:9-10 "Do not lie to each other, since you have taken off your old self with its practices and have put on the new self, which is being renewed in knowledge in the image of its Creator." Did you notice that the taking off and the putting on are both referred to in the past tense in this verse? This is a true mind shift. It is simply believing I am no longer that old man. The old is gone the new has come. I am a new creation in Christ Jesus.

Evidence of new nature living

"Outside in" living allows the old nature to continue to rule our lives. The Bible teaches us that in Christ we need never live "outside in" lives again but that we can live "inside out" lives just as God promised. We can walk in the Spirit and enjoy our new nature. We are not in bondage — to sin, to our old nature, or to worldliness.

God is not trying to get our old nature to **behave**, He is trying to get our new nature to **believe**. This is why the dominant sin of the New Testament is unbelief. In Hebrews 3:12 we are told, "See to it, brothers and sisters, that none of you has a sinful, unbelieving heart that turns away from the living God."

We are empowered by the finished work of the cross to live holy lives, free from sin, enjoying intimacy with God and living life to the fullest.

14

CHAPTER FOURTEEN

YOU ARE ONE WITH CHRIST

So far we have settled a few issues. We have seen that we are always forgiven, dead to sin, have the gift of righteousness, and have a new nature in Christ Jesus. It is time to settle another issue: we are in permanent union with Christ - independent of our behavior.

I am in perfect union with Christ

I'm not sure about your church background, but like many Christians I was taught that my sin separated me from fellowship with Christ. I grew up believing that God had somehow done some heavenly bookkeeping and He erased my sins, but in real life my behavior determined my fellowship with Him. If we think about this carefully, we realize how absurd this notion really is. Are we saying that once we have accepted Christ we move in and out of fellowship with Him based on our performance? Is that the plan that the Father had in mind before the foundation of the world? That He would "sort of" reconcile us to Himself? He is far more loving and far more committed to us than we could ever understand. It is His kindness that brings people to repentance — it is not His judgment that does so. Romans 2:4 says, "Or do you think lightly of the riches of His kindness and tolerance and patience, not knowing that the kindness of God leads you to repentance?"

Once more we have to separate the old covenant from the new covenant. Under the old covenant the Spirit of the Lord came upon people for specific causes or periods. In the Psalms, you see David crying out to the Lord, "Do not cast me away from Your presence and do not take Your Holy Spirit from me" (in Psalm 51:11). This is the old covenant relational structure. Behavior translated into presence. Behave and the Lord will not cast you away from His presence nor take His Holy Spirit from you.

Under the new covenant however, God says, "Never will I leave you; never will I forsake you" (Hebrews 13:5). In fact, He says that nothing in the seen or unseen world can separate you from His love, "Who shall separate us from the love of Christ? Shall trouble or hardship or persecution or famine or nakedness or danger or sword? . . . No, in all these things we are more than conquerors through him who loved us. For I am convinced that neither death nor life, neither angels nor demons, neither the present nor the future, nor any powers, neither height nor depth, nor anything else in all creation, will be able to separate us from the love of God that is in Christ Jesus our Lord" (Romans 8:35-39).

God has removed the power of sin that separated you from Him. And now that you have been reconciled to Him, nothing in all of creation can change that. God knew that the only way in which you could be a temple of the Holy Spirit and host His divine presence was that you be perfectly righteous and holy. No exceptions! As we discussed previously, we have all discovered that none of us can attain that state, so Christ on our behalf redeemed us to Himself and made us righteous by free gift. We are now the holy saints of the Lord - temples of the Holy Spirit. Think about that for a minute. He is the Holy Spirit. He can only be hosted in a holy place — a holy temple. That is you!

What happens if we sin?

God does not count your sin against you. He calls you to live a holy and righteous life worthy of your new status. If you make a mistake doing this, what is His solution for you? Does He say that you should confess your sins some more and make yourself righteous? Does He say you must restore fellowship with Him because now it's broken? What does the Bible really say we ought to do? Let's look more closely at 1 John 2:1, "My dear children, I write this to you so that you will not sin. But if anybody does sin, we have an advocate with the Father--Jesus Christ, the Righteous One. ... I am writing to you, dear children, because your sins have been forgiven on account of his name."

Wow! John is saying that we should not sin, but if we do sin we are comforted by the fact that we are already forgiven on account of His name. All our sins have been accredited to His account and all His righteousness has been accredited to ours. We know that Jesus Christ the righteous one is our advocate with the Father. He is our attorney who steps up and says, "All those sins are no longer on her record — they are on mine and my righteousness is now on her record" Praise God!

I am hidden in Christ

Your life is hidden with Christ in God according to Colossians 3:3. It's a double layer. First you are hidden with Christ and together with Christ the two of you are hidden in God. That is a pretty permanent state of affairs wouldn't you say?

The reason this is so important is it dramatically affects our thinking. If we're constantly trying to earn our way into right standing with God, we are functioning under an old covenant mindset. But under the new covenant, we have relational security in Christ purchased by His own precious blood. When the Father implemented His grand plan before the foundation of the world, it was a perfect plan designed to permanently and completely restore you to himself.

God or not God

If you have a philosophical bent, perhaps this illustration may help. Imagine a circle that represents all that God is. The circle has boundaries because God has boundaries. God cannot be unfaithful, He cannot lie, He cannot be unloving, and He cannot contradict Himself. In His perfect being He's contained within this enormous circle. Everything outside of that circle is not God. When Lucifer, who was "in God," rebelled he moved outside of that circle and became part of "not God".

We were born in the "not God" area and Jesus came and reconciled us through His own sacrifice and made us part of God again. How do we think we can so easily slip out of being part of God? Are we saying that sin is more powerful than the blood of Christ? Do we earnestly believe that the work on the cross was not complete and that it depends on us to complete it? You have new covenant thinking, so you understand the permanence of the work of the cross, the completeness of the work of the cross and most importantly that you are now in a perfect union with God.

Neuroscience shows that when people feel safe there is a different chemistry in their brains. Even in a work situation, if people are fearing losing their jobs and feel they need to defend their position, they have an entirely different brain chemistry designed to defend themselves. This is a very stressful state of mind and not very healthy at all. However, if people feel safe an entirely different chemistry is released in the brain and people find it much easier to be innovative, positive and intentional. This is a very healthy state for any person to work in. (Simon Sinek calls this the "Circle of Safety" in his book *Leaders Eat Last*.)

In the same way, if you are not secure and safe in your relationship with Jesus, you have an entirely different brain chemistry when you relate to Him. If you settle in your heart once and for all that you are in a permanent and secure relationship with Jesus, your brain will function very differently when you relate to Him. Instead of feeling condemned, unworthy, and the need to constantly apologize, you come to Him boldly and enjoy all the benefits of being a son or daughter. You are a friend of Jesus and not a servant. Jesus himself said so, "I no longer call you servants, because a servant does not know his master's business. Instead, I have called you friends, for everything that I learned from my Father I have made known to you" (John 15:15). If Jesus does not call you a servant, you certainly do not have the right to call yourself that. He means for you to feel safe and secure in your relationship with Him so that you can confidently step into the future He has for you! He redeemed you into His Circle of Safety.

Irreversible union

This union with Christ is irreversible. There are those who question and ask about the verse that speaks of "falling from grace"? So let's take a look at that verse. In Galatians 5:1-4, "It is for freedom that Christ has set us free. Stand firm, then, and do not let yourselves be burdened again by a yoke of slavery. Mark my words! I, Paul, tell you that if you let yourselves be circumcised, Christ will be of no value to you at all. Again I declare to every man who lets himself be circumcised that he is obligated to obey the whole law. You who are trying to be justified by the law have been alienated from Christ; you have fallen away from grace."

Starting in verse 1, we can see the point of the entire chapter is about the fact that Christ has set us free. Paul is telling us to stand firm and not allow ourselves to be burdened again by the law. Verses 2 and 3, Paul is saying that there is no value to obeying the law (allowing yourself to be circumcised) and in fact if you do that then Christ is of no value to you at all. He's saying that if you choose to start obeying the law then you have to obey the whole law, and if you do that you have fallen from grace i.e. you have made Christ to no effect. This verse is not talking about Christians losing their salvation. It is talking about Christians who have entered into the new covenant of grace and then chosen to go back to the old covenant. Paul is saying that when we try to blend the old and new covenants we make Christ of no value. The gospel of the new covenant is Jesus plus nothing. Jesus plus anything is no gospel at all.

This means that you accept the new covenant based on faith from first to last and add nothing to it. Look at Romans 1:17, "For in the gospel the righteousness of God is revealed--a righteousness that is <u>by faith from first to last</u>, just as it is written: 'The righteous will live by faith'". This is a very radical issue throughout the new covenant — that a different kind of righteousness is revealed that is by faith from first to last.

There is a clear warning for us under the old covenant. We learned earlier that the law cannot make anyone righteous or help anyone be a better person. We learned that the law points us to Christ. Once we have accepted Christ we can never again go under the law. Paul's stern warning in Galatians 5 is that we need to stay free in Jesus and not subject ourselves again to the law or we will make Christ of no effect in our lives.

Paul shows the security in Rom. 5:1, "Therefore having been justified by faith, we have <u>peace with God through our Lord Jesus Christ"</u>. What wonderful news! We now have permanent peace with God through our Lord Jesus. It says clearly that this peace comes through Jesus and we access it by faith. It does not say that we have peace with God as long as we maintain fellowship with Him through our good behavior and confession of sin. It is not our works that create this new status of permanent peace with God - that would never work for anyone, anywhere, at any time. It is by faith alone that we are fully justified. Now it is time to be at peace with God from this day forward — never again to look in the rearview mirror but to drive our lives forward knowing that we are in permanent good standing with our heavenly Father. He made a way for us when we could find no way. He is just that kind and that good!

CHAPTER FIFTEEN

REVOLUTION OF GOODNESS

On my 21st birthday, I had an extraordinary experience of unexpected goodness. I grew up in a home where we were taught the value of hard work and earning money. My first car, for example, was a tiny Toyota pickup that my father's company had driven into the ground. Its engine was blown, and the bodywork was full of dents and in a sorry state. I sold my motorcycle and several other possessions to be able to buy this old pickup. With the help of a friend, I pulled the engine out and completely rebuilt it. We fixed the bodywork and re-sprayed the car which we did in a driveway so you can imagine what the paint job looked like! Not a pretty sight but was a huge improvement on what it was. I even bought a new Toyota sticker to put on the back. This was my car for a good portion of my university life.

I had about 40 friends over celebrating my 21st birthday and as we came to the end of the evening, my father told me that our neighbor across the street wanted to do a toast at his house. I was irritated that our party had to be interrupted by an interfering neighbor. I remember thinking, "Why does he make it about him when this is supposed to be my big day?" Since my father was insistent, we stopped the music and moved the entire party across the street. It seemed absurd having all of us packed into his small kitchen. Again, I was irritated and wondered why we could not use the living room. Did this guy not know how to entertain guests? After the toast with us all standing in the kitchen, my father opened the back door that was attached to the garage and told me that he could hear some knocking and that I should go and open the garage door. None of this made sense but I went anyway. To my enormous shock a beautiful new VW Jetta with ribbons all over it stood in the garage. I was so stunned and confused. My father and mother with great joy in their faces, called out "happy birthday son!" It took me several seconds to compose myself and for the realization to hit me that this was my new car!

I don't know if you've ever had such an experience. It is truly overwhelming and the effect lasts for a long time. All that talk about going over the road was all a ruse to get me to my gift. I was so happy. All my friends were cheering and shouting. It was truly a life-changing event. I had no expectation that my father would ever do such a thing for me. He had made me work for everything in my life.

I drove around in my new car enjoying every moment of it. I think it took months for me to believe that it was truly mine.

The reason this was life changing for me was that I learned a very deep lesson: there are wonderful things in life that you receive that you did not earn. It is a good thing to teach children to earn and to work hard. It is a way to prepare them to be successful in life.

I remember discussing the whole surprise with my dad the next day. He told me that I sat in his office and picked up the brochure for the Jetta that the dealer had left on his desk. He said I read the brochure and put it down. At that moment he thought the game was up and that I had guessed what he was up to. I don't remember ever touching that brochure and the thought certainly never entered my mind. I was so convinced that something like that would never happen to me.

I raised my own children in the same way. Anyone familiar with the parenting courses that Bridget and I have done, is familiar with our views on the matter of teaching children the value of money and responsibility. (For more information go to www.4-11.org).

The problem of hard work

The problem of this approach is that there is little space for children to understand unmerited and unearned favor. While they were growing up, from time to time I would give them unexpected money and, of course, they were surprised and enormously grateful.

While at high school, my oldest son, Bruce, decided to take on a janitorial position to help build his savings so that he could buy his first car. I loved his attitude and approach. But, I started to notice a change in him. It seemed like he was learning that life is hard and that he should not expect any help from his father. Yeah I know - I was thinking, "Bad father, bad father!"

It is a problem firstborns have to endure, their parents learning how to be parents. During our parenting seminars we often joke by saying, "Our firstborn suffered from severely disabled parents."

My wife and I prayed about how we could address this seed that was growing in Bruce's heart. I must also say that this was a time of difficult financial stress for our family and I had limited options. The Lord reminded me of that new car I received on my 21st birthday and what it did for me. When you've worked for everything, great gifts are an enormous blessing. I felt the Lord tell me that I should buy him a new car — not just any car but the specific one that he had been admiring.

Round number 2

As Bruce graduated from high school, we organized a graduation ceremony — with a difference. At that ceremony we announced to all our friends and family that our parenting was officially over and that Bruce was now a man in his own right. I took time to type out a father's blessing which I read to him. As a group we prayed for him and blessed him.

Leading up to this event, I had a friend of mine "borrow" Bruce's old car, which coincidentally was also a Toyota. We took the car to the local dealership and traded it in for a brand-new car.

We had carefully positioned the new car in the garage and it was my daughter's sole mission throughout that evening to ensure that Bruce stayed away from the garage. As we concluded the ceremony, I told Bruce that I had a little surprise for him. I told him that we had lied about borrowing his car, and that I'd taken it in for a service and had all the repairs done as a way to celebrate his graduation. I also told him that we had it carefully detailed and that the car came out looking like a completely different car. In Bruce's normal way, he was full of gratitude and thanks. I invited him to step into the garage and take a look. I cannot describe to you the shock and look on his face staring at that new car! He seemed to laugh and cry all at once. All the friends cheering and congratulating him made the event so special.

After everyone left, Bridget and I explained to Bruce that this car was to help him understand that God's love towards him was not based on his performance. God had led us to buy this car so that every day when he drove in it he would remember that he has help from his Father whether he deserves it or not.

The gift to Bruce had the exact effect we had prayed for. I had to set expectations for the other three children that this was not the new norm for them when they graduated. I explained that we would seek the Lord on what to do for each of them. We have always believed in loving each of our children uniquely and not having worldly thinking in our love toward them. When my next two children graduated we blessed them with different gifts as we were led by the Lord. We look forward to our youngest (Luke) graduating to see what the Lord will lead us to do for him.

Expecting God's goodness

I told those stories to illustrate how good gifts can change our perception of ourselves, of our world and of the Lord. The Scripture wants us to understand that every good gift we receive comes from our heavenly Father. In James 1:17 it says, "Every good and perfect gift is from above, coming down from the Father of the heavenly lights, who does not change like shifting shadows."

This is wonderful news! The Bible tells us that the Father does not change His mood towards you like a shifting shadow. The Father is always in a good mood concerning you. He loves you and, like a good and perfect Father, loves to give you good and perfect gifts. Jesus said, "If you, then, though you are evil, know how to give good gifts to your children, how much more will your Father in Heaven give good gifts to those who ask him" (Matthew 7:11 NIV)

Time to upgrade our view of God's goodness

It is time for us to change our view of our heavenly Father. We must go beyond worldly thinking in which we think that God the Father is like our own earthly father. From your inner being, the Holy Spirit is sending you the deep thoughts concerning who the Father is.

Leif Hetland (the Norwegian minister known as the ambassador of love) once said, "When you believe in Jesus you are saved but when you believe that Jesus believes in you, you are transformed".

How God's goodness works

As we've seen many times in this book so far, we get a limited perspective when we read the English Bible. For example, this word "good" in English has a far deeper and more wonderful meaning than we may think when we simply read the English word. 1 Peter 2:1-3 tells us that we can change the way we think and talk as we drink spiritual milk which helps us grow up in our salvation. Interestingly, the growth is caused by experiencing God's goodness. It says, "Therefore, rid yourselves of all malice and all deceit, hypocrisy, envy, and slander of every kind. Like newborn babies, crave pure spiritual milk, so that by it you may grow up in your salvation, now that you have tasted that the Lord is good."

There's that word again — "good". It's translated from the Greek word *chrēstos* which has two distinct elements: 1) something that is useful, helpful in a practical way, and 2) pleasant or kind. When we've experienced God in this way, that He has been helpful in practical ways and it has been pleasant to us, we have experienced the goodness of God.

It is God's kindness that leads people to repentance. Take a look at the Scripture in Romans 2:4 NIV, "Or do you show contempt for the riches of his kindness, forbearance and patience, not realizing that God's **kindness** *[chrēstos]* is intended to lead you to repentance?"

It is not God's judgment that brings people to repentance, but His goodness — that is both pleasant and helpful. God's goodness is often experienced through the kindness of others. It is fascinating that Jesus asked us as believers to treat all men (believers and unbelievers) with this kind of goodness.

An easy yoke

You may be surprised to learn what Jesus meant when He said, "For my yoke is easy [chrēstos] and my burden is light" (Matthew 11:30 NIV). That word in English "easy" is the same Greek word chrēstos - God's goodness experienced in a helpful and pleasant way. Jesus was saying that He wants us to personally experience God's goodness in a helpful and pleasant way so that we can share that same experience with others. He made it clear that this "burden" is really no burden at all. It is, in fact, "light".

Helpful and pleasant

A few years ago, I walked into a restaurant in Europe and was commanded by the server to sit down. My order was taken with military precision and perfectly executed. The server was most helpful but most unpleasant. It was great service done with the finesse of an army general.

Living in the South, people place a high value on kindness which makes living here wonderful. Southern hospitality is well known and very pleasant to experience. Living in Atlanta, Georgia I've come to expect a certain pleasant interaction all the time. When you travel to other parts of the country or other parts of the world people can seem rude and unpleasant by comparison.

But what good would it be if someone who needed my practical help received a pleasant word from me but no help. It would be like a poor person approaching somebody getting out of their new car and asking for help to get food to eat. What if the response was, "Well aren't you a wonderful person? Have yourself a wonderful day — stay warm and well fed." That would be a pleasant interaction but of no use whatsoever to the hungry person.

Freely give what you freely received

You can only give what you have received. Jesus told us to freely forgive others because we've been so freely forgiven. The way of the Kingdom is: we freely give because we freely received. The problem as we've talked about in previous chapters, is that we do not spend enough time receiving and therefore have limited amount to give others. When you think about God's enormous patience with you and how much of His patience you have received, how could you possibly be impatient with others. But if we have never spent time thanking the Lord for His patience and kindness towards us, our hearts are not filled with His love and gratitude. We are meant to flow from the inside out. As we receive from the Holy Spirit, we overflow to others around us.

Drink more

If you find yourself being impatient with others, the solution is not to try harder to "be more patient." The answer is to take a moment and thank the Lord for His enormous patience towards you. Drink in of His goodness — His pleasant practical help and love. You will find a new level of genuine patience flowing from your heart towards others.

People who say they cannot forgive those who have hurt them, have not enjoyed the rich blessing of God's forgiveness. We can apply this to every aspect of our lives. Remember that Scripture encourages us that "we have received *everything* that we need for life and godliness." Any time you see a need or a shortcoming in your life, it is time to go and **drink from the fountain of life within.** It is time to get the river flowing from the inside out.

This is an immensely practical approach. You can receive from the Lord in the middle of a conversation or in the middle of a business presentation. You can receive from the Lord while you walk, talk, and go about your life. You can receive from the Lord while blessing your children or disciplining them. You can receive from the Lord while you are arguing with your spouse or asking the Lord to give you something sweet to say that will truly bless them. We are one with Christ and He invites us to allow His river of life to flow through us so that we can truly enjoy the life that comes from the fact that, "It is no longer I that live, but Christ to lives in me" (Gal 2:20).

Sharing God's goodness with others

Jesus sent you the Holy Spirit so that rivers of living water can constantly flow from your inner man to those around you. He wants them to experience God's goodness - His pleasant helpfulness. As you interact with others ask yourself: "Am I being pleasant and am I being helpful?" When you find yourself short in one of those two areas you know what to do — time for a drink!

Drinking from the Holy Spirit is a wonderful and simple thing to do. People often think that we are proposing a very advanced or sophisticated spiritual exercise. Nothing can be further from the truth. Walking in the Spirit is the most natural thing for any believer to do. You were made for this. You were designed to walk in fullness of life with the Holy Spirit in Christ and enjoying the love of the Father. This is the life God intended for you.

16

CHAPTER SIXTEEN

GOD IS RESTORING LIFE IN YOU

The plane began to taxi along the runway at Frankfurt International Airport. The passenger in 27A looked unusually nervous. I was seated in 27C. I watched as the plane took off for its direct flight to Atlanta, Georgia and noticed that my fellow passenger was beginning to sweat and look terribly uncomfortable. "Are you okay?", I asked. He looked at me nervously and asked if I had touched the newspaper that had been placed on the seat in 27B. He seemed petrified of it. As soon as the "fasten seatbelt" signs were turned off I rang the flight attendant call button and asked the attendant to remove the newspaper. Now I was intrigued. I introduced myself to my new friend and reached out my hand. He recoiled and looked frightened, staring at my hand like I'd offered him a vicious viper. I apologized and moved as far away from him as I could, watching him visibly relax. I had heard of obsessive-compulsive disorder before but had never encountered it in such an intense and direct manner. He introduced himself as John and apologized for his behavior explaining that he couldn't go anywhere near newspapers. It turns out that my new friend John was a very brilliant man who held two PhD's in particle physics. To put his mind at ease we started talking about his work and about physics in general. Having done three years of physics in college I knew enough to understand the very basics of his work. I love the subject and eager to learn, especially since the discussion seemed to put John at ease.

John was an American studying in Germany and working on some very cutting-edge experiments with an international team. I was fascinated. Physics has become so philosophical, and at times theoretical physics seems more fantastic than science-fiction. After my 2 hour physics lesson, I turned the conversation to the subject of God. "John, as a physicist, do you believe there is a God? Do you believe in an all-powerful being that created and manages the universe?" John looked at me as though I asked him if he believed that Mickey Mouse ruled the galaxy. "Of course not!", he said. This led to another two hours of my asking a lot of questions to understand John, while frantically praying for a key that could unlock his heart. It did not take long before the conversation turned to his early childhood which turned out to be very traumatic. At the worst point in his childhood, when he was deeply betrayed by his parents, he was holding a newspaper in his hands. From that day on the revulsion of newspapers was more than he could possibly tolerate.

I remember praying, "Jesus you are the way the truth and the life. Holy Spirit please show me the key that will help John find his way back to you." Throughout this book we've been talking about the fountain of life within, and how our minds can be ignited directly from Heaven with the deep thoughts that flow from God. A new thought came to me as clear as a bell and I turned to John and said, "I think I can see why the concept of God is such a difficult one for you. Everything you have said in the last few hours indicates that you believe that truth is divergent — that it starts with you and moves out into the universe in ever increasing complexity. The Bible says exactly the opposite. All truth converges on the person of Jesus Christ. It teaches that all complexity, all mysteries, all knowledge, and all things ultimately point to and resolve themselves in the person of Jesus Christ. That is why the Bible says Jesus is the way the truth and the life."

The remaining six hours of the flight led to a most wonderful and pleasant conversation. We listened attentively to one another as I introduced him to the extraordinary person of Jesus and listened carefully to his responses. I did not lead him to the Lord that day but as we landed in Atlanta he turned to me and said, "This has been one of the most helpful and encouraging conversations I've had in my lifetime."

God is on a mission. He plans to restore life to every human being. To those of us who've accepted him as Lord and Savior, He works to bring life into every aspect of our personality, character, thinking, emotions, and inner world. He is not interested in correcting the behavior of our old man. He fully plans to bring us the extraordinary and abundant life that comes from our new man.

To help us understand this process, I want to go back to the diagram we used earlier.

NOTHINGNESS
(Not God)

If Jesus is the way the truth and the life, then there is no life other than the life of God. It means that everything that is not God is nothingness. Nothingness is not a real thing — it is merely the absence of life. In the same way, we don't have elements called light and dark. We have light and the absence of light. We have given the absence of light the name dark. The difficulty with language here is that we think that darkness and light are two things that are the opposite of each other. In reality there is only one thing and that is light. For ease and convenience we have given the absence of light a name.

Life versus nothingness

The Bible explains that Jesus is the darling of creation. It says, "For in him all things were created: things in Heaven and on Earth, visible and invisible, whether thrones or powers or rulers or authorities; <u>all things have been created through him and for him</u>" (Col 1:16).

So, logically, Jesus is life — since all things have been created through Him and for Him. Nothing exists outside of Him. That is why the Bible says, "Jesus is <u>the</u> *life*." This is a powerful key to unlocking the life of God in each of us. It means that when something is lacking in us, that lack can be filled with the life of God.

Let me explain it this way: when I'm with my best friend (my wife) I enjoy her fellowship and her friendship. When she goes on an extended trip I desperately miss her fellowship and I feel loneliness. Loneliness is merely the word we give for the absence of fellowship. Loneliness is, in and of itself, part of *nothingness*. All *nothingness* can be replaced by the *life* Jesus so abundantly provides. I can enjoy His fellowship at any time and replace the *nothingness* (loneliness) at will. This is a profound idea that can dramatically transform our lives.

Everything the world offers is based on *nothingness*. It does not contain *life* since all *life* is in Jesus. So what the world calls "fun" is just packaged up *nothingness*. It is fascinating that every person experiences this as *nothingness*. People often talk about getting home from a party and feeling the emptiness and meaninglessness of it all. In an attempt to fill the *nothingness* and to get rid of it from our lives, the human race has invented extraordinary distractions and entertainments.

It is true and sad that many believers experience *nothingness*. When we say we are depressed we are really saying we have no joy in our lives. Once again we have given the absence of joy a name — depression.

Do you know this riddle?

What is more powerful than God, more evil than the devil, poor people have it, rich people need it, and if you eat it you will die?

Nothing! Nothing is more powerful than God, nothing is more evil than the devil, poor people have nothing, rich people need nothing, and if you eat nothing you will die.

This fun little riddle holds some biblical truth. Romans 8:13 says, "If you live by the flesh you will die." If you feed yourself on nothing you will die. Now it starts to make sense that Jesus offered to bring us *life* and *life* in abundance.

Jesus offers you *life* when the world offers you *nothingness*. That is why it is so critical to understand the finished work of the cross. Because it is the cross that sets us free from worldliness and sin. In short, the cross sets us free from *nothingness*! Jesus offers *life* and life in abundance in every area of our lives. It is up to us to allow the fountain of *life* within us to flood our inner being. We can let the *life* of God flow through us - healing us of every depression, anxiety and fear.

We are called to a life of faith. Faith releases the *life* of Godthrough us and affects every area of our lives — it transforms our thinking, it ignites our emotions, it directs our will, it keeps us free with a clear conscience. Now that is true living.

I recently heard Graham Cooke ask a simple question, "Did Jesus do a perfect work on the cross?" The obvious answer is "yes!" He went on to ask, "If Jesus did a perfect work on the cross on your behalf then He has dealt with the old man and made you a new man, correct?" Now perhaps you may answer, "Yes - um I think so." Graham asked his third and key question, "What if there is nothing wrong with you but something is missing?"

This is an interesting approach to the gospel. It takes God's word at face value and draws the very logical conclusion that if Jesus did a perfect work on the cross and that you were indeed crucified with Christ, then you were raised in newness of life with Him — just as the Bible says. If you are indeed a new creation — all the old has passed away — all things have been made new. The only logical conclusion is that there is nothing wrong with you, but that there are things missing.

This ties in perfectly with our discussion. The only thing the enemy can do is to keep things from you, i.e. offer *nothingness* to you. The peace of Christ is yours and therefore you simply need to let it reign in you. The Bible says, "The joy of the Lord is your strength." All the fruit of the Spirit is designed to fill the *nothingness* the enemy attempts to provide.

"But the fruit of the Spirit is love, joy, peace, long-suffering, kindness, goodness, faithfulness, gentleness, self-control. Against such there is no law. And those [who are] Christ's have crucified the flesh with its passions and desires." (Galatians 5:22-24 NKJV)

When you came to Christ, the passions and desires of *nothingness* (those not of God) were crucified with Christ. Notice the Scripture puts this act in the past tense, "Those who are Christ's **have** crucified the flesh". It is not our job to kill the flesh. Jesus did that for us at the cross. It is our job to walk in the newness of *life* He provides.

The fruit we are talking about is not our fruit. This fruit belongs to the Spirit. When we allow the *life* of God to flow through us — the fountain of *life* to flow — the Holy Spirit with all His attributes flows through us. Notice that it is not the "fruits" but the "fruit" of the Spirit. This means that the Holy Spirit brings us a quality of life that transcends any meager human passions and desires. God is not asking you to learn self-control or gentleness. God is offering you self-control and gentleness as part of an overall package that will flow through your life as a by product of the Holy Spirit's presence in you.

Praise God that it is not up to us to try to imitate the fruit of the Spirit and to create a worldly invention that mimics each of these elements. We are set free from the human self-effort to create an anemic version of love, joy and peace. We are offered the real deal — free of charge — fresh from Heaven. We are offered love, joy and peace which contains the very *life* of Jesus Himself. All the world can do is package up *nothingness* and attempt to deceive us in the hope that we will not see through the ruse. What the world calls love, joy and peace is an illusion and a shadow used as wrapping paper for more *nothingness*.

The Holy Spirit is on a mission to redeem back every area of your life. He wants to make you just like Jesus! He intends for you to enjoy everything Jesus paid for at Calvary. The New Testament writers go to great lengths to tell us that there is no need for us to walk in the old man — to put off the old man and to put on Christ.

It is time to banish nothingness

The first key step to living an abundant *life* and allowing the fountain of *life* to flow through us, is to recognize that Jesus has already paid the price for us to enjoy His abundant *life*. The second step is to acknowledge that He has fully qualified us to receive our inheritance. The third step is to identify areas of *nothingness* in our lives — anxiety, fear, depression, lust, envy, hopelessness, etc. We can then boldly draw from God all that He has for us. By taking time in His presence and allowing the Holy Spirit to minister to us, the *life* of God will flow in us and fill every area of *nothingness* with His glorious life.

17

CHAPTER SEVENTEEN

WHY JESUS IS PRAYING FOR YOU

Jesus is praying for you. He is making intercession for you, creating a bridge between you and God. He is constantly doing this. The question is, why? Why does Jesus need to do this and what is His purpose for doing so?

Jesus is making intercession for you — but for what reason?

Many people can tell stories about somebody who prayed for them — a grandmother or parents who refused to give up on them. Heaven's population has been dramatically increased by such people who prayed for friends and family to accept Christ. Bridget and I have been very blessed to have parents who prayed for us. I will not be surprised when we get to Heaven to discover that many of our victories were due to our parents' prayers.

It is very encouraging to know that someone is praying for you. It is interesting that Hebrews tells us that Jesus is constantly interceding for us. "Therefore He is also able to save to the uttermost those who come to God through Him, since **He always lives to make intercession for them**" (Hebrews 7:25 NKJV).

But the real question is, what is Jesus interceding for? We have established thoroughly in our previous discussions, that Jesus took care of sin once and for all. So, if Jesus is not interceding for our sin, what is He interceding for?

It is true that when we sin or are accused by the accuser (Satan) that Jesus acts as our Advocate. He stands before the Father and removes all claims that the enemy has against us. All our sin has been fully paid for and therefore the enemy has no basis on which to accuse us. The Bible encourages us, not to sin, but if we do sin we can be encouraged by the fact that we have the most powerful Advocate in the universe removing all condemnation from our lives. "My little children, these things I write to you, so **that you may not sin.** And if anyone sins, **we have an Advocate** with the Father, Jesus Christ the righteous" (1 John 2:1 NKJV).

The issue of sin being absorbed by Christ explains His role as our Advocate but does not explain His role as our Intercessor. The key to understanding this role, is to continue reading 1 John 2. Look at what verse 5 and 6 says, "But whoever keeps His word, truly **the love of God is perfected in him**. By this we know that we are in Him. He who says he abides in Him ought himself also to **walk just as He walked.**"

Jesus is working with the Father to perfect God's love in us. When His love is perfected in us, we walk just as He walked. The rest of the book of 1 John shows us very clearly that the key to having Christ's love perfected in us is to receive His love. We already know that the key in the Kingdom of God is being a great receiver. Receiving God's love more and more perfects His love in our lives. When His love is perfected in our lives, we find ourselves easily loving others. Because we've so freely received the Father's love, we can freely give it to others regardless of their performance and behavior. The Father loved us while we were yet sinners. He loved us when we least deserved it. This unconditional love and kindness is what drew us to Him.

Jesus is constantly talking to the Father about you and about how to perfect their love in you. His love perfected in you will cause you to walk just as Jesus walked — to walk in your inheritance. This is God's plan for you: His love for you transforms you. As this love is perfected in you, you will be in this world just as Jesus was.

"In this the **love of God** was manifested toward us, that God has sent His only begotten Son into the world, that **we might live through Him**. In this is love, not that we loved God, but that He loved us and sent His Son [to be] the propitiation for our sins. ... And we have known and believed the love that God has for us. God is love, and he who abides in love abides in God, and God in him. **Love has been perfected among us in this**: that we may have boldness in the day of judgment; **because as He is, so are we in this world**. ... We love Him because He first loved us" (1 John 4:9-10, 16-17, 19 NKJV).

What does saved mean?

Let's break down what the Scripture is saying. When you came to Jesus you were saved. But this word "saved" has two parts to it: the first part means that God will make you **safe**, and the second part means that God will make you **whole**. That is why the Scripture talks about being saved in the past tense, the present tense and the future tense. The day you accept Jesus Christ as your Lord and Savior, you are made *safe* in God. He took all the consequences of your sin and set you free to live a powerful life in Him. But He means you to be saved to the uttermost — he wants to redeem every part of your life and make you *whole*.

"For the message of the cross is foolishness to those who are perishing, but to us who **are being saved** it is the power of God." (1 Corinthians 1:18 NIV)

Let's go back to the verse in Hebrews 7: "Therefore He is also able to **save to the uttermost** those who come to God through Him, since He always lives to make intercession for them."

The intercession that Jesus is making for your life before the Father is to save you to the uttermost — to see the Father's love perfected in you. Now that you've been made safe in your permanent union with Jesus, He means to make you whole and restore life to every aspect of your being. This restoration process is part of your inheritance in Christ.

You have been given a call from Heaven but that can only be accomplished when you live as Jesus lived. That in turn, can only be accomplished when His love is being perfected in you. That is why you have boldness in the day of judgment because you know you are safe in Jesus. (Love has been perfected among us in this: that we may have boldness in the day of judgment.)

Right now there is an invitation from Heaven offering you to step into your inheritance in Jesus. Jesus paid an extraordinary price at the cross to secure for you a glorious inheritance for which He has fully qualified you. Human tradition, externalized religion, worldliness, sin, and even the forces of darkness cannot keep you from this spectacular life.

Jesus paid the price on the cross and then takes it to a whole new level by permanently making intercession for you before the Father. How kind and awesome is that?

He means the Father's love to be perfected in you. He means for you to be **safe and whole**. The key to living in the world as Jesus did is to receive the Father's love into every area of your life. His love neutralizes all nothingness and energizes you with the *life* of Jesus.

18

CHAPTER EIGHTEEN

WALKING IN GRACE

We've covered a lot of material and I do not want you to become overwhelmed with all the detail. I provided the detail simply to show you that you are being offered a spectacular and glorious inheritance in Jesus.

Everything we've discussed so far was to show you that the Bible is offering you an abundant life. We explored the biblical inner man model to show how this would practically work and then we discussed the incredible aspects of the gospel of grace.

So far we've covered three big ideas:

1. Discovering the fountain of life within
2. How you are wired internally
3. A clear understanding of grace and the goodness of God

These three topics form a foundation. Once you have a clear understanding of grace, you are transformed from a works based focus to a Christ based focus. You are freed from trying to achieve what Jesus has already achieved on your behalf. Grace empowers you to step confidently into the finished work of the cross and access your inheritance in Christ.

Having a clear biblical inner man model, helps you to understand that you have access to the deep thoughts of God that can transform your thinking, your emotions, your will and your conscience. Grace enables you to have a biblical definition of yourself and to reject a worldly view of who you are. Your sense of self is informed by your spirit and the deep thoughts and revelation that flows from God. You are freed from allowing the world to define you. You find yourself believing what God says about you and jealously guarding any other definitions of yourself that do not align with this view from Heaven.

Once you discover that you have access to all the power of Heaven, through the finished work of the cross in Jesus, you find yourself stepping out boldly in faith. When you realize that your obedience to Christ is based on the fact that He has already given you everything you need for life and godliness, you see your calling and your purpose in life in a wonderful and inspiring new way.

Where is this leading us?

We want to take a minute in this chapter to talk about walking in grace. Grace leads us out of darkness, transforms our lives and empowers us to live a kingdom lifestyle. What does this mean? When you realize that you are truly forgiven, that you have been made righteous as a free gift from God, that you are dead to sin, that you are alive to God, that you've been given a new nature, and that you have been seated with Christ in heavenly places, you begin asking a different set of questions. You find yourself no longer focused on "not sinning" and on "obedience to the law." You start asking questions like, "How can I reach others with this wonderful gospel of grace?", "What is the purpose of my life?", "How can I bring Heaven to Earth today?", and "How can I walk in intimacy with Jesus and in the power of the Holy Spirit today?"

The purpose of all the material we've covered so far is to help you get past the focus on yourself and put the focus on Jesus.

Let's explore the typical things we think disqualify us from walking in the fullness of grace.

Disqualifier #1: I am not called to be full time

Strangely, when your focus is on Jesus, you find yourself reaching out to the world. We have notions that we have to be in "full-time" ministry before God can truly make our lives count for Him. Most people feel that they are not called to be a full-time minister and therefore feel disqualified to be useful to God. It turns out that every single believer is full-time and that God longs to make each of our lives count — to bring His love to a desperate and dying world. If you are in Jesus, you are His full -time person in the place where you work and live.

If you don't see yourself that way, it is time to upgrade your thinking. Just like you upgrade the apps on your smartphone, God is offering upgrades for your mind. He wants you to think like He thinks.

Disqualifier #2: I am waiting for my breakthrough

Many are waiting for a "breakthrough" before they can step out and truly be who God has called them to be. Perhaps you believe that you are not right with God while you have the struggles and problems that you're currently facing. Somehow you've come to believe that powerful living occurs once your challenges and obstacles are removed. This is simply not the case. You do not have to wait for your healing, restored relationship, financial breakthrough, emotional wholeness, new job, or clear calling from Heaven to enjoy God today. The invitation from the Lord is that you be available to Him today — that you accept His invitation to the abundant life you are being offered — even while you remain in crisis. You can serve God when you feel least capable and least qualified to do so.

Remember it is <u>His</u> life within you that brings transformation to others. You cannot heal anyone, restore anyone, redeem anyone or save anyone. You could not do that for yourself. It is a wonderful revelation to realize that <u>all transformation is God's responsibility.</u> Once you free your mind of self-performance, self-evaluation, self-analysis, self-righteousness, and self-importance, you find that you are free to live life to its fullest and to see God move through you in dramatic and unexpected ways.

Disqualifier #3: I don't live a powerful life so it is obviously not for me

Jesus sent the Holy Spirit so that you can walk in the power and truth of the finished work of the cross. He came that you may have life and life in abundance. The Holy Spirit's job is to lead you into all the fullness and truth of who Jesus is and the Father's immense love for you. The Father goes before you and prepares every good work for you to walk in. He has given you gifts and abilities to fulfill the purpose of your life. Jesus came and rescued you from the Kingdom of darkness and translated you into the Kingdom of his glorious light. The Holy Spirit is your guide, your friend, your counselor and will lead you into the fullness of the life for which you were destined.

The Lord uses every situation of your life to offer you an upgrade for your mind — to live the life Jesus promised and for you to become all He has called you to be.

The disciples in crisis

In Acts chapter 4, Peter and John were arrested because of a demonstration of the Holy Spirit's power — a lame man was healed. Religious people are often offended by the demonstration of power. In the story, we see Peter and John in prison and then brought before the religious leaders and questioned. The Bible tells us, "When they saw the courage of Peter and John and realized that they were unschooled, ordinary men, they were astonished and they took note that **these men had been with Jesus**. But since they could see the man who had been healed standing there with them, there was nothing they could say" (Acts 4:13-14 NIV).

Please get this: These were ordinary men that caused others to be astonished. These men were unschooled. Their education and schooling were not the qualifications for power living. What qualified them? The answer is right there in the verse: "these men had been with Jesus."

Being with Jesus qualifies you for power living

Just like Peter and John, we are called to walk in power and see miracles performed in the name of Jesus. Even religious leaders bound in their traditions and worldly thinking cannot refute a power demonstration. But if you look carefully at the story we just read, you see there was another power demonstration: Peter and John spoke with authority as the Holy Spirit enabled them. Even the religious leaders knew that this authority was not their own.

When you walk with Jesus you start to ask different questions like: "Jesus, what do you think about this situation? What are you seeing that I cannot see? What are **we** going to do about this?" It is the "we" part that causes us to step out in faith and trust God.

Grace leads us outside of ourselves and empowers us to bring Heaven to Earth. The next logical step is that we start to pray for the sick and expect God to do the miraculous.

Look what happens a few verses later after Peter and John had been released, they "went back to their own people and reported all that the chief priests and the elders had said to them..... they prayed, 'Now, Lord, consider their threats and enable your servants to speak your word with great boldness. Stretch out your hand to heal and perform miraculous signs and wonders through the name of your holy servant Jesus.' After they prayed, the place where they were meeting was shaken. And they were all filled with the Holy Sprit and spoke the word of God boldly. All the believers were one in heart and mind. No one claimed that any of his possessions was his own, but they shared everything they had. With great power the apostles continued to testify to the resurrection of the Lord Jesus, **and much grace was upon them all.**" (Acts 4:23, 29-33.)

Grace is more than power for salvation. It includes the power for all aspects of a supernatural life including of healing and miracles. Notice the last line in that story, "and much grace was upon them all." We must enlarge our view of grace. Grace is God's power at Christ expense that empowers you to live a powerful Christian life.

Transformed from powerless to powerful

The life of grace often starts when we realize that we are powerless to change our own lives. We discover that we do not have the power to modify our behavior to the standard the Scriptures require. We discover that God does not want us to teach the old man to behave. He wants the old man to die and for us to arise in newness of life. It is His desire that we rely 100% on His power to be transformed from the old to the new. We become new creations with the same resurrection power that raised Jesus from the dead. This is part one of the transformation Jesus intended.

We become powerful because we are in Jesus. At some point powerlessness ceases to define us. We become convinced that we are seated in heavenly places with Christ. We realize that it is not up to us to do miracles but it is up to us to allow His power to do miracles through us. Such boldness comes when we are convinced that we are not our own — that we are bought with a price. What freedom — when we realize that we belong to Jesus. What people think about us is nothing in comparison to what they think about Him.

Growing in grace

As believers, we never come to a point in our Christian walk when we can say, "I have enough grace." In fact, the Bible encourages us to grow in grace both individually and corporately as the church. We can be individuals who walk in little grace or in much grace. In the same way, we can be in churches with little grace or much grace.

"But **grow in the grace** and knowledge of our Lord and Savior Jesus Christ. To him be glory both now and forever! Amen" (2 Peter 3:18 NIV). This verse is interesting because it provides us with a powerful key to growing in grace. Notice that to grow in grace we also have to grow in the knowledge of our Lord and Savior Jesus Christ. It is sad when believers see Jesus as merely a means of salvation. After they accept Christ, Jesus fades into the background. But we are called to grow in our knowledge of Jesus. Notice that we're not being encouraged to know *about* Jesus but to know Jesus himself. As simple as this idea may seem, for many believers it is a revolutionary idea. We must **fall in love with Jesus** and grow in our passion and love for Him on a daily basis. He is the most extraordinary person in the universe — our heavenly Bridegroom.

How weird would it be, for a bride to get married and then show little to no interest in her new husband? She simply acknowledges him as having changed her last name and that she is now one with him, but makes no further effort to get to know him and grow in her knowledge of him. We would think that such a bride would need serious help and counseling. We must, therefore, be careful not to be that bride. We must **never lose our fascination with Jesus** - His act of love on the cross and His love toward us. We must get to know the person of Jesus, which is more than what He did for us on the cross. Our love for Jesus must continually grow. Our fascination with Him must increase.

It isn't enough to believe certain facts about Jesus - even Satan and the demons believe these facts (James 2:19), but they don't love Him.

Jesus is our sovereign Lord. When we obey Him we are acknowledging His lordship and His authority over our lives. Our obedience is driven by our love for Him. Jesus said (John 14:21) "Whoever has my commands and keeps them **is the one who loves me**. The one who loves me will be loved by my Father, and I too will love them and **show myself to them**."

The grace cycle

The more we love Him, the more we obey Him, the more He shows Himself to us, which causes us to love Him more, and the cycle grows in an ever more wonderful upward spiral.

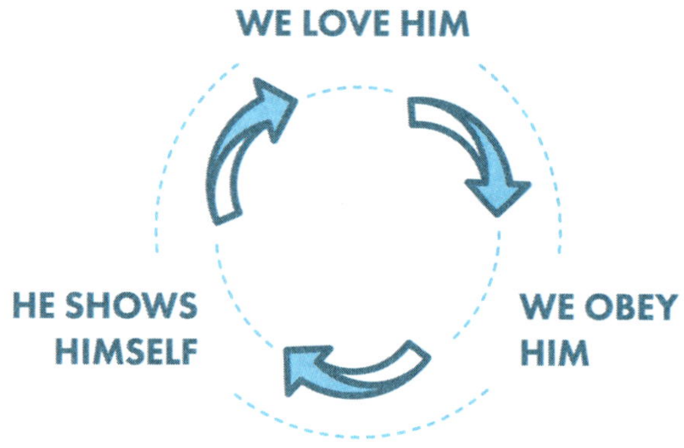

Growing in grace is about growing in our <u>knowledge</u> of Jesus and in our love for him.

Grace does not allows us to be passive

Grace empowers us to be active in our faith and walk in our inheritance. We must be careful of thinking that we can now be passive since everything was done for us at the cross. What was accomplished at the cross on your behalf empowers and authorizes you to walk with power in the kingdom.

Power of humility

The book of James provides us with another powerful key to growing in grace. It says that God gives us more grace and the key to receiving more grace is to be humble. Look what it says in James 4:6, "But He gives more grace. Therefore He says: "God resists the proud, But gives grace to the humble.""

So we put these two components together we find that humbly obeying Jesus is the key to increasing grace in our lives. As always, Bible solutions are so simple that a child can do it. These are not advanced topics for the spiritually mature, but these are the baby steps of obedience that launch us into a powerful journey of grace.

Like all new covenant truth, you are set free from your own self-righteous pursuits and encouraged to be your new self. Jesus holds us accountable to grace. He expects us to believe all that He did for us - to take it at face value. He wants us to be free and holds us accountable to stay free.

But what about all the time I've wasted?

Perhaps you were not clear about grace before and now you feel you wasted so much time living under the yolk of the law. There is really good news for you.

Jesus addressed this issue by telling a story about different laborers coming to work in a field at different times. He explained that some workers were there at 6 AM in the morning, and that throughout the day different workers came at different hours. The last group of workers arrived one hour before the end of the working day. As the workers lined up to receive their wages, those who came early assumed that they would be paid more and were shocked to discover that everybody received the same wage. They were furious and contested it. The owner of the field simply said that it was his money and he could pay people however he liked. He had honored the agreement with each group of workers.

For a long time I hated this parable. Probably because I assumed that I was one of the 6 AM workers. I was speaking to the Lord about this one day when He said to me, "Son, the reason you don't like the story is because you do not understand the power of redemption. Some will learn truth early in their lives and they will receive the full reward of that truth, but some will learn very late in life. For those who come at the last hour, I will redeem the time and make it so that they end their lives as though they had learned the truth early on." I was blown away by such kindness. The Lord is truly the kindest person you will ever know. How kind of Him to make up and redeem time for those who have lost it?

If you have been caught up in sin, worldliness or externalized religion, God can redeem the time. The wonder of His grace is that all who come to Him are fully satisfied. All who call on the name of the Lord shall be saved and redeemed.

It is time to make a radical decision

You can decide that from today on, you will rest from your own self-righteous efforts and accept by faith the finished work of the cross on your behalf. When we rest from our own works and accept Jesus' work on our behalf, we find peace with God. It is amazing how many believers do not have peace with God even though the Scriptures say, "Therefore, having been justified by faith, we have peace with God through our Lord Jesus Christ," (Romans 5:1).

The remainder of this book is all about redeeming the time. Now that we understand the gospel of grace, we are in position to take our first steps into walking in grace. All inheritance in God is achieved from a place of rest. We will learn to see things as God sees them, think about things like He thinks about them, speak about things like He speaks about them, and then step out in courage and faith.

In the next chapter, we are going to introduce the incomparable Holy Spirit. He has been assigned by the Father to guide us into all truth and be the primary means of how we grow in grace and walk in the Spirit.

10

CHAPTER NINETEEN

MEET MY FRIEND, HOLY SPIRIT

I want to invite you to go with me on an imaginary trip to the most extraordinary conference ever held in the history of mankind. What makes this conference so special is the keynote speaker: the Holy Spirit - God Himself. Now, I am quite sure you can imagine that tickets to this conference would be extremely rare and difficult to get.

The reason I have tickets for the two of us to attend is that I have been given the extraordinary privilege of introducing the keynote speaker. I've been practicing this introduction for months, but somehow everything I write seems weak and anemic in comparison to the beauty of His person. Can you help me? Do you know him? Can you think of an appropriate way to introduce Him?

As we drive to the conference, we review my introduction. I hope you can add to it. I'd like to practice, please tell me if you think this works:

"Welcome ladies and gentlemen — brothers and sisters in the Lord. (Pause) In all the history of mankind, no audience has been so privileged as to welcome our next keynote speaker. His very words create life and they will utterly transform you.

His accomplishments include: the creation of the universe; the author of Scripture; and bringing power to the church of Jesus Christ. He is currently employed by God the Father to make Jesus glorious and transform people from the Kingdom of darkness into the Kingdom of light.

His job includes being the deposit and guarantee of our salvation, our guide into all truth, our all-powerful intercessor, the revealer of mysteries, our all-knowing teacher, and the perfect comforter of all mankind.

He has been awarded many well deserved titles. He has been called the Spirit of truth, the Spirit of life, the Spirit of glory, the eternal Spirit, the Spirit of holiness, the Spirit of knowledge, the Spirit of understanding, the Spirit of the fear of the Lord, and the Spirit of grace.

(Pause) ... and now ladies and gentlemen, prepare for the most spectacular revelation of the very nature of God. Please welcome, the kindest person you will ever meet, my very dear friend, the Lord - Holy Spirit!."

Is He welcome?

What kind of welcome do you think He would receive? He walks onto the stage with a huge smile beaming out to the whole crowd. His love, joy and peace radiates from the center of His being. The entire auditorium lights up with the ecstasy of His presence. The crowd is on their feet cheering and shouting and screaming. The applause is deafening, making all applause, ever to be given in any stadium anywhere, seem feeble by comparison. The Holy Spirit stands at the podium, waiting for the ecstatic crowd to calm down. Life radiates from Him, feeding the deepest area of every soul in the stadium. But instead of the meeting calming down, it seems to erupt with wave after wave of love and joy, while igniting explosions of more rounds of applause. It's the most incredible experience imaginable. Healing is flowing into bodies. Doubt and anxiety fizzle into insignificance in His glorious presence. With every wave of healing comes more rejoicing. He hasn't even opened His mouth yet and people are being set free from pain, deep emotional wounds, traumatic conditions, and every human ailment flees in His presence. As people are liberated and set free, their hearts well up with the warmth of His love and the liberty of His joy. It's a 2 Corinthians 3:17 moment, "Now the Lord is the Spirit, and where the Spirit of the Lord is, there is freedom."

Everyone in the stadium is experiencing a freedom and liberty that surpasses their personality and personal inhibitions. Each person is instantly convinced of God's deep love for them. They are liberated by His joy - knowing they have complete peace with God, and He hasn't said anything yet. He's just standing at the podium loving each person individually and loving us all corporately — all at the same time. It is absolutely wonderful.

His idea of church

The Holy Spirit is so magnificent and so wonderful. This is His idea of church. When He is welcomed in a meeting as Lord, people's lives are transformed. Why on Earth would we ever try to downplay His presence in our meetings? Why would we ever disregard His Lordship and treat Him like a topic, or a force, or an option? Why would we possibly treat the book He wrote as having higher authority than Himself? What could possibly make us afraid of His love, His peace, and His joy? Why would we not allow ourselves to be caught up in praise and glorious worship in His presence? Why would we withhold anything from such a wonderful person? What are we so afraid of?

Externalized religion has taught us to be fearful of exuberant expressions of worship. While they glorify intellectualized Christianity, they mock what they do not understand. If that is what you grew up with and what you were taught, I have glorious news for you: God wants you to be free. He wants you to enjoy the abundant life of Jesus in you.

It is time that we silence these cold lifeless ways in our hearts and surrender to the Lordship of the Holy Spirit. We must learn to trust Him. He is Lord. He is not an optional topic but an incredible person you need to know. He is loving, kind, funny (hilarious actually), and so much fun to be with. He lives in you. Learn to know Him more.

His invitation to you

The Bible invites us to be continually filled with the Holy Spirit (Eph 5:18). There are so many more verses commanding us to be filled with the Holy Spirit. It is interesting that these references use a specific Greek tense which could be translated as, "be being filled with the Holy Spirit." It is an active, constant offer that we be continually filled with the Holy Spirit.

The Holy Spirit is the means by which grace flows through us. When you accepted Christ into your life, it was the Holy Spirit who did the work of bringing you into Christ. It is by His power that the full benefit of the cross is activated in your life.

He is the member of the Godhead that executes according to the Father's will. The Father said. "Let there be light." Since all things were created through Jesus and for Jesus, the Holy Spirit made it happen.

Hearing God's voice

There are parts of the body of Christ who are very comfortable with the idea of hearing God's voice and they have trained themselves to hear better, the longer they have walked with God. But there are those who regard such an idea with suspicion and are afraid of "hearing voices." Some say this is even a dangerous idea since people will stray from God's Word and fall into error.

We learned in earlier chapters that we have a spirit in constant "download mode" - receiving from the Lord constantly. So, how then do we hear God's voice?

You can train your mind to look into your spirit and see what's there. Your mind uses its natural language to describe what it sees. The natural furnishings of your mind is the language you will use to describe what is in your spirit.

Let me give some examples of this. If you are an engineer, you will likely use engineering terms and ideas when decoding what you are receiving in your spirit. Let's say that you are asking God if you should take the new position that your firm is offering you. This new position requires you to move to a different city. You pray and get a sense of something forming in your mind. You may say. "I feel like God is showing me a bridge that I need to walk over. It is well secured because He made it and it is safe for me to move into this next opportunity. It feels strong and solid." As you speak, you feel peace building in your heart. You know the Lord is speaking to you.

It is always necessary to check what you have heard with the Scriptures and with spiritual people you trust. God never contradicts His own Word and He can further confirm your leading through others.

Let's rerun the previous example and assume you are an artist. You see a new picture being painted with bold colors and you see it in a strong frame. You feel God encouraging you to be bold and see into this new picture which He is framing as a solid option for you.

God uses your internal language to speak to you. The deep thoughts of God flow from your spirit into your mind. It is a good idea not to mix that with worldly thinking and talk yourself out of what the Lord is leading you to do. Perhaps the new job is less money even though it is more aligned with what you want to be doing. You could be tempted to follow the money and not the Lord. Conversely, just because a new opportunity means more money does not mean it is from the Lord.

Some years ago a close friend received a job offer in a new city. He prayed and after he heard from the Lord he asked if we could discuss it. He shared that he did not feel a "go" or "stay " from the Lord. Instead He felt the Lord say that is was his choice and that either way God would bless him. This was very different from my own leading to move to Atlanta. Even when, in my darkest moments of cultural adaption, I pleaded with God to send me somewhere else, He held firm, "You are called to Atlanta." My friend shared with me what he felt God was saying to him. While listening something in my spirit felt the rightness of it. He chose to move and accepted the new offer. After accepting the new offer, he called to tell me that he felt peace and the Lord's pleasure with his decision.

Our will and God's will

We often assume that God's will is opposite to our will. Many think that if it's something they want then God will want them to do the opposite. There are times this is true - even for Jesus when He prayed in the garden before His crucifixion when He asked the Lord to remove the burden from Him but added, "Not my will but your will be done."

When we choose to do what the Lord is leading us to do, it leads us into an upgrade in our thinking. It puts us on the path of our calling and moves us directly into our inheritance.

When you submit your will to His, you are creating alignment with Heaven and His power is released into your life. More grace is released. You grow in your knowledge of Him and you understand more of His character.

The role of the Holy Spirit

Our entire relationship with the Lord is managed and governed by the Holy Spirit. We discussed how we hear God's voice and His leading. These are the functions of the Holy Spirit. Remember the Scripture in 1 Cor 2:10? It says the Holy Spirit searches the deep things of God for you and then reveals them to you. As you seek Him so He reveals these deep things to you.

This is the Holy Spirit's job description from the Father. He is to reveal to you as much as you press in to know. The more you seek, the more you find. "Seek and you shall find." You may feel that you are doing this on your own but every step is led by the Holy Spirit. The more you recognize Him and what He is doing, the more you can cooperate with Him. You were designed for relationship with God. Every aspect of your being is designed for fellowship with Him. Your entire being is meant for God - Body Soul, Heart and Spirit.

Living in a house with God

You are a temple of God designed for His holy habitation. It is not His plan to visit you on occasion. You are not an orphan but His son or daughter. It is an orphan spirit that makes us think the the Lord wants to visit us from time to time. He has made a way for us to dwell with Him in constant and permanent habitation. There are times we have special moments of intimacy with Him. Our habitation hosts these type of intimate moments. He does not leave us after we have enjoyed a sense of His presence. He is always there.

It is our **awareness** of His presence that changes, not His presence itself.

Let's use an illustration for this. I live at home with my wife. We do life together and we dwell in the same house. We have moments of intimacy too. These intimate moments are hosted by the fact that we have a covenant and dwell together.

The same is true of you and God. You are His beloved. He has a covenant with you in Jesus. He has made a way in Jesus for you to permanently dwell with Him and to enjoy moments of encounters with Him.

How weird would it be if I arrived at home and my wife met me at the door and said, "You are most welcome here husband." I'd reply, "Of course I am welcome here, I live here!" (I'd wonder what was wrong with her to give me such a strange welcome.)

We must be careful of an orphan spirit that begs God to be welcome in our meetings when He lives there. We know He is there because we brought Him in. We are not orphans coming to church on Sunday hoping to catch a glimpse of our Father. We live with Him and dwell with Him. We host His presence.

Both Psalm 15 and 24 talk about dwelling in His holy hill. Like the climbing example I used at the beginning of the book, we are not expected to climb and perform our way into His presence. He has placed us at the top of the mountain - permanently in His presence because we are now hidden with Christ in God.

Doing life with God

He wants to do life with you in every aspect of it. He wants to replace all the nothing spaces with His Life. Who has been assigned to manage this process in you? You guessed it. It is the Holy Spirit.

He is so wonderful. You can speak with Him, discuss things with Him and even joke with Him. He has a fantastic sense of humor. I am sad to say that only in the last few years have I discovered how playful the Lord can be. Somehow, my theology did not permit it. It seems that all my communication was serious. I have slowly learned that He is playful indeed - in a really kind way. He does not cause pain or destruction and "play" with us. That is not at all what I am talking about. I am talking about learning what things He finds funny and how He loves to tease.

Holy Spirit's creativity

One morning I was exhausted even though I just had 8 hours of sleep. I was feeling a little discouraged and in a low energy mood. I was talking to the Lord about it saying, "Lord, sorry I am not with it this morning. I'd love to hear from you."

"Sure," He said, "here is what I want you to do. There is an excellent sermon that I want you to watch. It will bless you and transform your mood. I have been saving it for today."

"Holy Spirit, that is so great," I said. "How do I watch it?" He said I should go to our own church website and He would show me which one. When I found the one He pointed out, I laughed. It was a sermon I had preached. "Are you sure, Lord?" I asked.

"Oh yes, " He said, "It's very deep - it will bless you." I heard Him laugh - not in a mocking way but in a way that was filled with excitement. I watched my own sermon in which I talked about learning to walk in the Spirit. Through the sermon, the Holy Spirit kept piping in "Deep," He said teasing me. I saw the funny side and started laughing. The more I laughed, the more He pressed on with comments, "Such an anointed man," "Such insights." On and on it went - Him teasing me kindly and me laughing. I laughed so hard my stomach hurt. He knew exactly how to appeal to my sense of humor. I cannot remember when last I laughed so hard. After 45 minutes of laughing in my bedroom, I gained enough self control to head off to my office. I was in an entirely different mood. My joy was restored and strangely so was my strength. I should not have been surprised since the Bible teaches us that the joy of the Lord is our strength.

A few days later, I was telling a friend about the experience and I almost lost it again! I could see that he did not see the funny side. It was one of those "you had to be there" types of funny. For weeks after I still giggled when I thought of that morning and the things the Holy Spirit said.

This may not sound very funny to you but He knew exactly what I needed and in His great kindness encouraged me in a very creative way. He will do the same for you. We need to upgrade our thinking of how we believe He wants to interact with us. Surely, it should be His choice? All too often our experience of Him is so limited that we neither expect such experiences or have been taught to be suspicious of them. There is a new invitation from the Holy Spirit to be constantly filled with Him in new and creative ways.

Expand your experiences with the Holy Spirit

If you are conservative, like me, you may want to experiment in private. Most of the powerful encounters I have had with God have been in private. It means a great deal to me that the Lord enjoys them as much as I do.

Here are some ideas on how to experience the Lord in new ways. In your bedroom or another place you know to be private, try one of the following:

1. **Sing a new song.** Ask the Holy Spirit to help you make up a new song and then sing it to Him. He does not mind if you are tone deaf and cannot keep a tune. You will be amazed by what is released in you when you try it.
2. **Shout for joy.** This may seem weird but try it. The Scripture tells us to shout for joy. I found that if I will forget my beloved dignity and do it, something wonderful happens: His joy is released in me. Maybe I misunderstood what "shout for joy" means. Perhaps it means that if you are joyful then shout, but I think it also means if you want joy, shout to get it. Shout for joy!
3. **Dance**. Don't knock it until you have tried it. I think I am the worst

dancer in the world but He loves it. He does not mind my poor attempts. He loves that I am experiencing Him in a new way when I obey the Scripture that tells me to dance before the Lord.

4. **Read Scripture to the Lord.** I love to read Scripture aloud to God. It provides a different experience of His presence.

There are many more I could suggest but you need to find them for yourself. Here is a hint: Read the psalms and do what they say.

This entire chapter has been dedicated to the idea that you were designed to have more grace flowing though your life which is accomplished when you get to know the Holy Spirit and His ways.

20

CHAPTER TWENTY

FREE YOUR MIND

We have made a great deal about the fact that we are made the righteousness of God by faith. We've seen in the scriptures that we have been given a new nature. To complete the picture we need to look at the idea that you can actively step into all God has for you. You can train yourself to walk in your new nature in Christ.

I Tim 4:7 says we are to train ourselves in godliness. Notice that we are made righteous by free gift - Jesus did that for us - but it is our job to train ourselves to be like God (i.e. godliness). We are to be like Him.

Activated for works of grace

Because of grace we can do the works of grace. Paul said in 1 Corinthians 15:10, "I worked harder than all of them--yet not I, but the grace of God that was with me." God's grace activates our lives for service and for fellowship. We function *from* grace not *for* it.

I have an access card to get into my office. Without it I cannot get into the building and therefore I cannot do my work. Christ gives you complete access to everything in Him so you can do the Father's work.

How it works

Let's go back to the inner man model. This time we're going to focus on how these components work together.

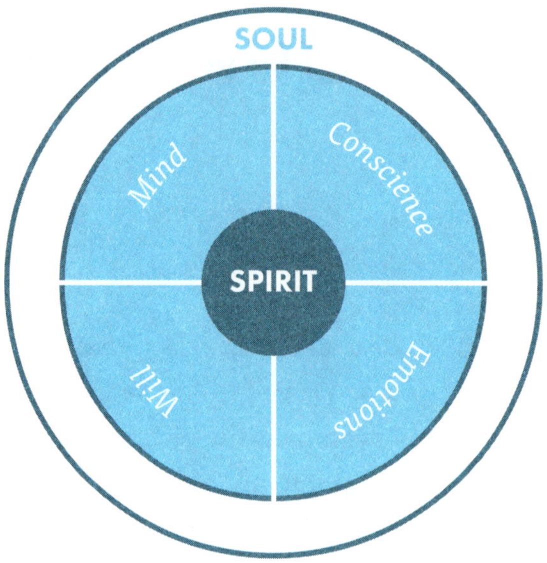

The mind of Christ

We're going to remove some of the components for the sake of clarity and give us the ability to focus in on specific elements.

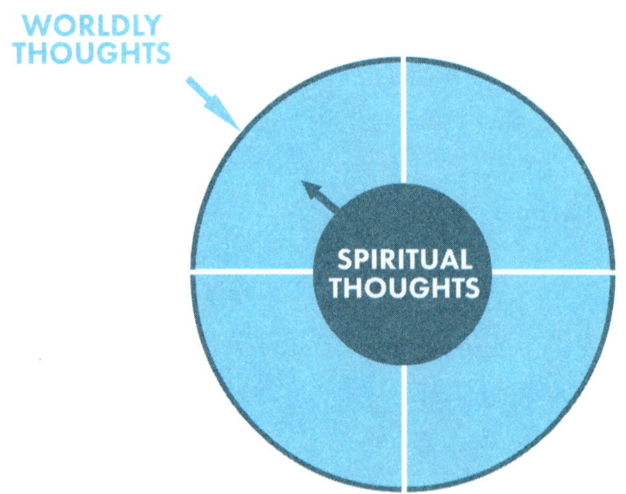

In a previous chapter we discussed the idea that the deep thoughts (dianoia) from the Holy Spirit flow from our human spirit into our minds. The world presents us with its thoughts and its way of thinking. Our job as believers is to renew our minds. We are to develop spiritual thinking and move away from worldly thinking.

I believe that the ministry of the Holy Spirit to the church worldwide right now is to teach the church heavenly thinking. Worldly thinking is the prime mechanism that strips believers of their inheritance in Christ. Conversely, spiritual thinking releases the life of God in us and creates alignment with Heaven. It all begins with thinking right not with doing right. Every day we get to choose whether we will receive the deep thoughts of God from our inner being or mimic the way the world thinks.

The Bible tells us that we have been given the mind of Christ. This makes sense since we know we were given a new heart the day we came to Jesus. Since the mind is part of the heart we know we were given a new capability of thinking. The mind of Christ in you must now be filled with the thoughts of Christ and not with worldly thoughts.

It may be helpful to think of the mind as a bowl and thoughts as water being poured into that bowl. You are given a new "bowl" - the mind of Christ when you are born again. It is now inappropriate to pour worldly thoughts into that new bowl, but it is entirely appropriate and indeed life-giving to allow that bowl to be filled with the thoughts of Christ. This is the part that requires our training. This is why we are told to train ourselves in godliness. We must learn to think like God thinks.

In Isaiah 55:8 it says, ""For my thoughts are not your thoughts, neither are your ways my ways,' declares the LORD." This verse is often misquoted as the reason why we have worldly thoughts and can never know God's thoughts. This is not what the Scriptures are teaching.

The verse before it says, ""Let the wicked forsake their ways and the unrighteous their thoughts. Let them turn to the LORD, and he will have mercy on them, and to our God, for he will freely pardon. 'For my thoughts.......'"

The Scripture is commanding us to forsake unrighteous and worldly thoughts and to turn to the Lord. This turning releases God's mercy into our inner world. This is an Old Testament picture of a New Testament reality. Like all scriptures in the Old Testament we have to filter them through the cross to understand what they mean in the new covenant. The Scripture in Isaiah clearly shows us that if we will turn to the Lord and align our lives with His thoughts we release all of God's blessing in our lives. The rest of the verse shows us that such thinking releases the rain of God that causes everything to grow. The power of these words then accomplishes all He intended to accomplish in our lives. It says, " ... As the **rain** and the snow come down from Heaven, **and do not return to it without watering the Earth and making it bud and flourish**, so that **it yields seed for the sower and bread for the eater**, so is my word that goes out from my mouth: It will not return to me empty, but **will accomplish what I desire and achieve the purpose for which I sent it**" (Isaiah 55:7, 10-11 NIV).

This blessing has already been purchased for you by Jesus. In fact, Paul says empathetically that "all things are yours." Here is an abbreviated version of 1 Corinthians 3:20-22, "'The Lord knows that the thoughts of the wise are futile. ...... All things are yours, ... the world or life or death or the present or the future - all are yours."

It is time that believers walk in this abundant life and enjoy the "all things are yours" way of living. It all begins with the thoughts that you entertain. This process begins with a very simple question we can ask of the Lord, "**Lord how do You see this?**" The Lord loves to teach us to think like He thinks. We learn how He thinks by reading His word and being led by the Holy Spirit.

The think test

Does the Bible tell us how to do this? Absolutely! Let's take a look at Philippians 4:6, "Finally, brothers and sisters, whatever is true, whatever is noble, whatever is right, whatever is pure, whatever is lovely, whatever is admirable--if anything is excellent or praiseworthy--think about such things."

We need to become actively aware of the thoughts that are in our minds and apply the think test by asking, "Is this thought true, noble, right, pure, lovely, admirable, excellent, or praiseworthy?" If the answer is yes to any one of these eight elements, the thought passes the think test.

Some may read this and think that this is an impractical way to live. Perhaps you're a little skeptical that such a high standard of thinking is possible. Some may say, "I have to focus at work on what I'm doing so I can provide for my family." Providing for your family is an admirable and praiseworthy thing. Focusing on your work easily passes the think test. We will talk more about this later.

Taking every thought captive

"What about negative thoughts. How do I control these? I find my mind filled with unhealthy thoughts," you may ask. I have excellent news for you! The mind of Christ you now have is a very powerful weapon. In fact, you have **authority over every thought** that is not in line with the knowledge of Christ. "The weapons we fight with are <u>not</u> the weapons of the world. On the contrary, they have divine power to demolish strongholds. We <u>demolish arguments</u> and <u>every pretension</u> that sets itself up against the knowledge of God, and **we take captive every thought** to make it obedient to Christ" (2 Corinthians 10:5 NIV).

Let's visualize this:

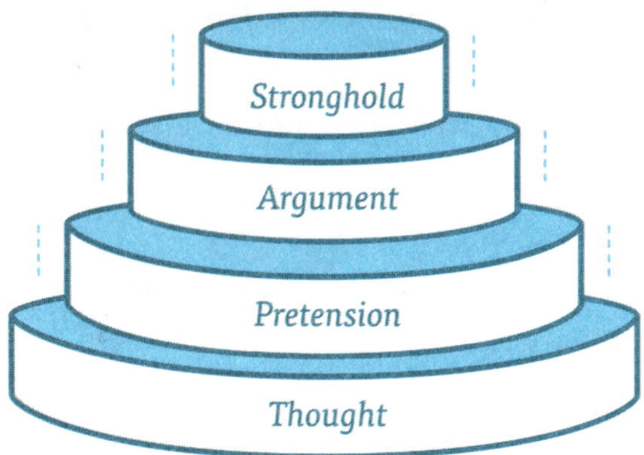

This verse goes straight to the top of the heap - strongholds. It says we have the power to demolish strongholds. Notice that this weapon is not of this world - it is not worldly. You cannot control worldly thoughts and strongholds with worldly weapons. You need divine power to deal with worldly thoughts. Great news: you have been given the mind of Christ that wields divine power to take every thought captive. The enemy can take years to build strongholds in your mind and in a few seconds it can be demolished by the divine power you now have. You are not a victim of strongholds! You are the victor!

Like this:

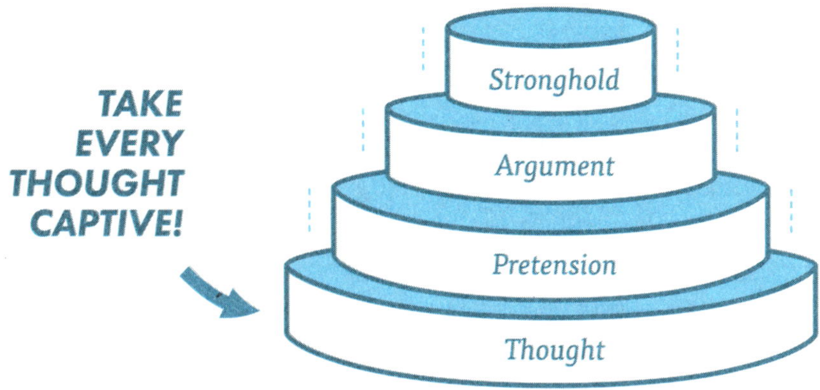

You have the authority to take captive every thought and make it obedient to Christ. This means that you can make the deep thoughts the Holy Spirit is giving you, the ones that win in your mind. The deep thoughts of God can be the ones that are the dominant thoughts in your mind. That is why the Scripture refers to worldliness as "pretensions." This is false wisdom pretending to be real wisdom. Have you ever noticed that when you spend time thinking about negative things you develop an argument inside your own mind? You can demolish these arguments and these pretensions because you have the mind of Christ. You have the power to take every thought captive in your mind and bring it into submission.

Demolishing strongholds

Negative thoughts are toxic to your mind and your entire body. We know from the latest neuroscience research that toxic thoughts literally poison the cells in your body. Stress and anxiety release cortisol in the brain which is toxic and causes cloudy thinking and toxicity in the body. We know that such toxic thoughts can lead to health problems and even serious diseases. This is why stress is such a destructive issue.

When we entertain worldly thoughts and pretensions, they develop into arguments in our minds. If we give these arguments enough attention, over time they can become strongholds in our lives.

How outrageous that a believer should suffer any strongholds when Christ has paid fully for their freedom. The reality, however, is that many believers live with strongholds in their lives. You cannot use worldly weapons to control worldly thoughts. You cannot expect that worldly strategies can deal with worldly thoughts effectively. It takes divine power released from a heavenly weapon to deal with negative strongholds in your mind. Negative strongholds can hold believers captive even though they have no right to do so and even though the believers have a power weapon to demolish them. It is time for believers to wield their mighty weapons and take these negative strongholds down! It is time for all believers to be free.

Being mature and complete

God cares about what you think because He wants you to be mature and complete - lacking nothing. To get there, you have to begin to think as He does. To help you with that, he wraps upgrades (like upgrades to your apps on your phone) in trials. These challenges are designed to deliver an upgrade to your thinking. When you understand this, James 1:2-4 makes more sense, "**Consider it pure joy,** my brothers and sisters, whenever you face trials of many kinds, because you know that the testing of your faith produces perseverance. Let perseverance finish its work so that you may be **mature and complete, not lacking anything.**"

You are enrolled in your Father's Mature-and-Complete Program. Worldly thinking focuses on "why is this happening to me" rather than "what is God doing for me?" Very different thinking right? I counsel people all the time who are focused on what is being done to them by others, rather that what is being done for them by the Lord.

The Lord is upgrading your thinking so you can be complete and mature. Now that is something to be excited about. You can count that as pure joy. That is spiritual thinking.

Don't be double minded

We are confused when we ask God for something and we do not receive it. Sometimes the reason is that God is waiting for His timing. Sometimes we are the cause.

When we try to mix worldly thinking with spiritual thinking we become double-minded. You cannot please the Lord with worldly thinking. He is kind and patient and will keep sending you the same challenges until you upgrade your thinking.

James explains this clearly in the next few verses (James 1:5-8), "If any of you lacks **wisdom** ***(heavenly thinking)***, you should ask God, who gives generously to all without finding fault, and it will be given to you. But when you ask, you must believe and not doubt, because the one who doubts is like a wave of the sea, blown and tossed by the wind. That person **should not expect to receive anything from the Lord**. Such a person is **double-minded** and unstable in all they do."

James is giving us a beautiful key. He is saying that we can ask God for heavenly thinking at any time (wisdom) and that God will give it generously without any condemnation or finding fault. We know Jesus has already fully satisfied the wrath of God so we can enjoy the favor of God. You need to grow up and become mature. God is fervently committed to your development. He uses every situation in your life to provide you with an upgrade. He turns every negative into a positive. All things work together for your good. Even curses are turned into blessings. Wow!

Some people believe they have been cursed. Some think they inherited this from their parents or grandparents. That is only true until you accept Christ. Jesus became a curse for you on the cross so you can be free and blessed. Every curse has now been reversed into an equivalent blessing.

You cannot mix spiritual thoughts and worldly thoughts. That does not qualify as an upgrade. So if you find yourself repeating the same lesson over and over, then it is time to take the upgrade. It is time to ask God for His wisdom on the matter and then take every negative thought captive. Free your mind to think as He thinks.

Now that you realize you are equipped with such a mighty weapon in God, you are free to think the wonderful extraordinary thoughts that God has towards you. He is passionate about who you are and who He has made you to be.

God is in a good mood towards you all the time! You are free from an old covenant theology in which God's mood toward you is determined by your behavior. You now walk in the favor of God because you're in Jesus. Remember everything that was due you was taken by Jesus on the cross. Everything that was due Jesus has now been put on you. You now walk in the kindness, goodness, and favor of your heavenly Father!

21

CHAPTER TWENTY ONE

LIVING A WORRY FREE LIFE

Do you know that Jesus expects you to live a **worry free** life? Do you know that He made a way for this to be true for you? Do you know that He created a way for you to deal with your problems so that your **mind can be free** to think positive and creative thoughts? It's all true. The gospel keeps getting better and better, doesn't it?

Jesus said that we are not to worry about our lives. He said in Matthew 6:25-34, "Therefore I tell you, **do not worry** about your life, what you will eat or drink; or about your body, what you will wear. Is not life more than food, and the body more than clothes? Look at the birds of the air; they do not sow or reap or store away in barns, and yet your heavenly Father feeds them. Are you not much more valuable than they? Can any one of you by **worrying** add a single hour to your life?

He added that worry about our lives is worldly thinking - pagan non-Christian thinking.

Let's keep reading that verse, "If that is how God clothes the grass of the field, which is here today and tomorrow is thrown into the fire, will he not much more clothe you--you of little faith? So do not worry, saying, 'What shall we eat?' or 'What shall we drink?' or 'What shall we wear?' **For the pagans run after all these things**, and your heavenly Father knows that you need them. But seek first His kingdom and His righteousness, and all these things will be given to you as well. Therefore **do not worry about tomorrow**, for tomorrow will worry about itself. Each day has enough trouble of its own."

Jesus commands us **not to worry about our life and not to worry about tomorrow**. Would your life change dramatically if you did not worry about your life and not worry about tomorrow?

Well, Jesus adds more. He says, "When you are brought before synagogues, rulers and authorities, **do not worry about how you will defend yourselves or what you will say**" (Luke 12:11).

Jesus says: "Do not worry about your life, tomorrow or how to defend yourself". Got it!

Paul takes it to the logical conclusion. You guessed it. Paul says do not be anxious about **anything**! Let's be honest. Most of us dismiss this as impossible. We see this as impractical and non-sensical. I found myself thinking this too until I dropped this type of worldly (pagan) thinking and upgraded to heavenly thinking.

What helped me do that was the verse in Philippians 4:6-8, "**Do not be anxious about anything**, but in every situation, by prayer and petition, with thanksgiving, present your requests to God. And the peace of God, which transcends all understanding (nous), will guard your hearts and your minds in Christ Jesus. Finally, brothers and sisters, whatever is true, whatever is noble, whatever is right, whatever is pure, whatever is lovely, whatever is admirable--if anything is excellent or praiseworthy--think about such things."

This passage of Scripture consists of three keys. Let's discuss each one so that you can upgrade your thinking too.

1. Bring your problems to God in prayer

You need to handle all problems at a spiritual level not a mental level. Every situation you find yourself in can be managed through prayer, not through worrying. If you trust that God has got your issue firmly in His hands you will let it go out of your hands. You will not let something go unless you believe it has been taken care of. So, the first part of the upgrade is to believe God has your situation in His hands. By faith you trust Him. You bring your requests to Him (petitions), and thank Him for the upgrade that is hidden inside this situation. It is like opening candy in a wrapper. The situation is the wrapper and the upgrade is the candy - the reason we count it all pure joy.

Here is a diagram to help you visualize this way of thinking:

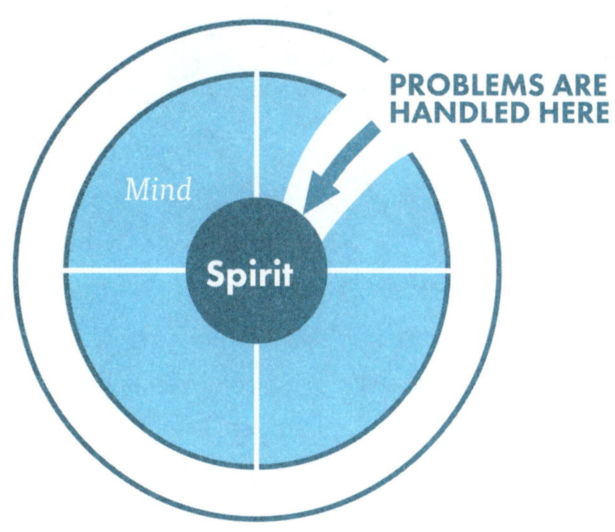

2. Protect your heart and mind

The second key to the upgrade is: "And the **peace of God**, which transcends all understanding *(nous - mind)*, will **guard your hearts and minds** in Christ Jesus." You keep praying and giving thanks until you release His peace. Remember we have been given the authority to let His peace reign. This peace will act as a shield to protect your heart and mind. Your mind is now freed from negative thoughts and protected to think positive thoughts.

We can add a protective layer around the heart to visualize this:

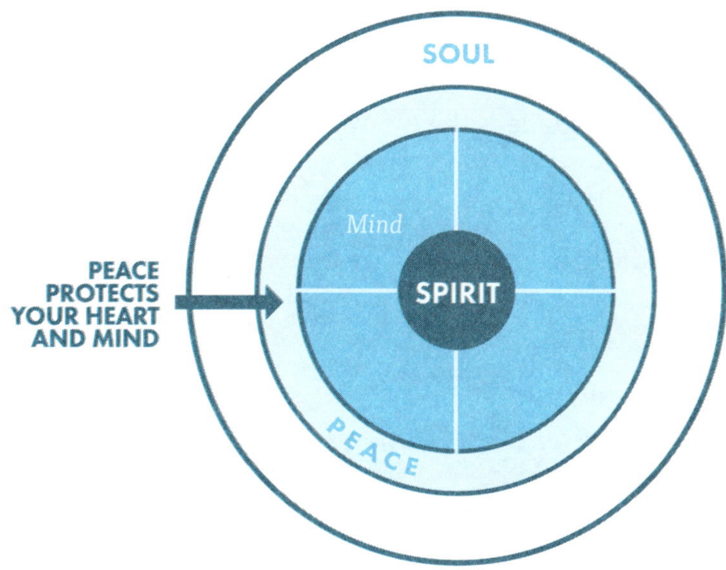

3. Think positive thoughts

Finally, brothers and sisters, whatever is true, whatever is noble, whatever is right, whatever is pure, whatever is lovely, whatever is admirable--if anything is excellent or praiseworthy--think about such things." You are now free to think positive thoughts, and your heart and mind are protected in that state.

Welcome to the upgraded thinking!

It is time to enjoy a free mind

Strongholds are removed from our lives when we start to protect our thinking. If a thought does not pass the think test, it can be disallowed. You have authority in Jesus to demolish strongholds. God has given you special spiritual weapons that are not like the weapons of the world. Your weapons have divine power. It takes divine power to bring your mind under control. Realize that when you take negative thoughts captive, you set your mind free. Remember it is for freedom that Christ has set you free (Galatians 5:1). **Jesus paid for you to have a free mind**. It is the thoughts of God - the deep thoughts - flowing from your inner man that that set you free. When you start to think about how much God loves you, how much He has forgiven you, how precious you are to Him, you become free in your mind.

The think test is a very broad framework in which our minds can enjoy freedom. Some may look at the verse in Philippians and think that this is a very narrow spectrum of thought. Nothing could be further from the truth. We could dedicate an entire book just listing the things that fit into the true, noble, right, pure, lovely, admirable, excellent, and praiseworthy categories. Some people have a very narrow definition of what constitutes spiritual thoughts. A simple way to define this is that all thoughts are holy and righteous except for sinful and negative ones. It is time to declare war on your own negative thoughts. It is time to wield the mind of Christ and win this war.

I strongly encourage you to memorize these eight elements. To help with this, you may want to group these eight elements into three categories that spell TAP. Open the TAP to let the life of God flow in you:

- **True** (noble, right)
- **Admirable** (excellent, praiseworthy)
- **Pure** (lovely)

True thoughts

I am amazed at how many believers spend time thinking about things that are simply not true. We all do this. We worry about our problems instead of thinking about God's faithfulness. We feel disqualified to ask God for anything even though God has fully qualified us in Christ. That is why I spent so much time in this book covering the foundations of grace and the new covenant. I had to lay a foundation of truth so that we knew what things to think about. If we don't know what is true, we do not know which thoughts to take captive. It is vital as believers to know the truth about who we are in Christ and oppose all thoughts to the contrary. It is imperative that as believers we know that we have been forgiven once for all! Any accusation or condemnation is a lie. These lies can be taken captive and forced to surrender to the knowledge of Christ - the truth that we have been forgiven. If we know the truth that we have been seated with Christ in heavenly places, we know that we are not victims of circumstance. We are able to step out in faith and trust God, because we know the truth - He is always faithful.

Admirable thoughts

There are many things we can think about that are not admirable. We have a modern society that fixates on superstars, but many of these superstars lives are not admirable. As believers we honor the honorable and we dishonor the dishonorable. The way we dishonor the dishonorable is to give things that are not admirable no mind space. As believers, our mind space is dedicated to things that are both true and admirable.

Pure thoughts

The last category is that of purity. All sexual impurity begins as a thought. We can take captive any thought that is not pure. Your mind is a sanctuary. It is designed to bring life to every aspect of your soul. We have the authority to remove pollutants - toxic thoughts that are impure and unlovely.

Taking control of your thought life

We have seen in this chapter that the Bible emphatically states we have the mind of Christ, and provides us with divine power to manage and control the thoughts that are in our minds. We have learned the thoughts that pass the think test (TAP) are the ones that bring us life and set our minds free. When we allow our minds to host negative and toxic thoughts, we restrict the power of God in our lives and may inadvertently stifle our inheritance in Christ.

You are now equipped with this powerful weapon - a weapon from Heaven - that can break the thought strongholds in your mind and bring every thought captive to Jesus' way of thinking.

Protecting your free mind

You now have a spiritual way of thinking which sets your mind free to live the way Jesus meant for you to live.

Perhaps we can visualize it like this:

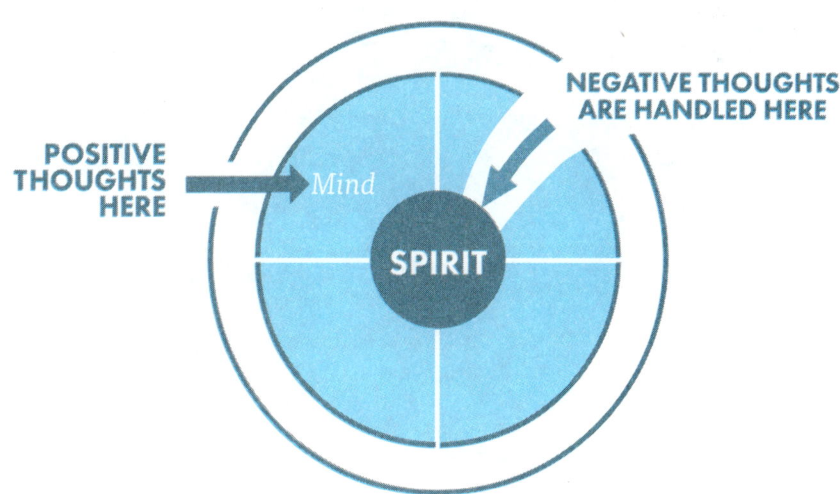

We honor the Lord when we live in freedom in our minds.

22

CHAPTER TWENTY TWO

GOOD THOUGHTS RELEASE LIFE

Building on the idea that good thoughts release God's life in us, let's take another look at our diagram:

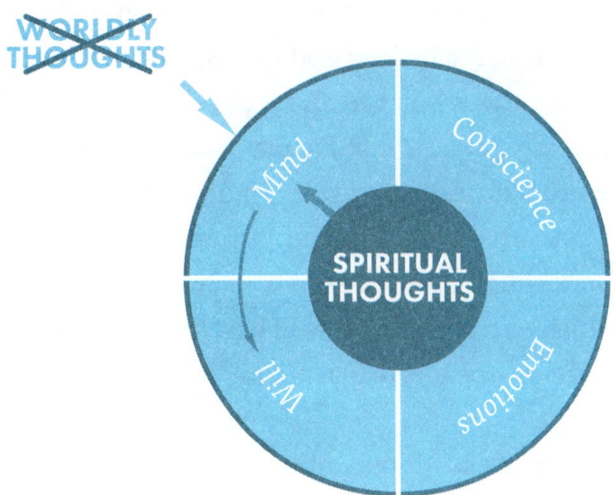

Thoughts lead to action

Thinking leads to doing. Good thinking leads to good actions and bad thinking leads to bad actions or inaction.

One of my most prized traditions in our family happens around my birthday. Bridget invites our children to our home and the celebration consists of each family sharing their testimonies of the year. We've encouraged each of our children to write down everything God has done for them throughout the year. Bridget and I had 96 testimonies in 2015! As we listen to all that God has done for each of our family members, we are blessed and a deep gratitude wells up in our hearts. It fills our minds with TAP thoughts. We think about the truth of His faithfulness and His kindness. It is truly wonderful to review in one sitting all that God has done in the entire year. Testimonies teach us to think correctly about God and encourage us to take faith-based actions.

Be bold

Some of the greatest feats of our heroes are recorded in the stories in the Bible. One of these is the story about Joshua. We know that God led the Israelites out of Egypt, through the desert, and into the promised land. Interestingly, they could have entered the promised land 40 years earlier had they chosen to believe God and be bold. Do you remember when they sent out the 12 spies to check out the land? This happened shortly after leaving Egypt. Only Joshua and Caleb believed God and were willing to be bold and courageous. Finally, when Israel approached the promised land, the Lord prepared Joshua to lead them into their inheritance. In Joshua 1:6 the Bible tells us what God told Joshua, "Be strong and courageous, because you will lead these people to inherit the land I swore to their ancestors to give them."

Once again, we see an Old Testament truth reflecting a New Testament reality. Jesus has purchased an extraordinary inheritance for us and it takes courage and boldness to take possession. It takes tremendous courage to believe God in the face of "overwhelming evidence" to the contrary. As believers we have the freedom to acknowledge the facts as they are - even if they are terrible facts. In the midst of a crisis the Lord is not asking us to pretend to be blind to the problems. He is asking us to acknowledge the facts exactly as they are and to trust Him regardless. It pleases the Lord when we act in faith rather than react in fear. He loves it when we courageously face down the enemy and refuse to budge. We stand firm on the freedom Christ purchased for us and simply refuse to move. This is being bold and courageous!

The Bible reminds us in Galatians 5 that it is for freedom that Christ set us free, and tells us to stand firm. Standing firm takes courage and confidence that God will never leave you nor forsake you. Standing firm requires faith. We also know from the Scriptures that it is impossible to please God without faith. God loves us to presume on His goodness and His faithfulness because it is impossible for Him to be unfaithful. He cannot lie - it is an eternal impossibility. When He says that He has forgiven you - it is true. When He says that He will never leave you or forsake you - it is an eternal truth.

In the previous chapter, we saw that powerful thinking releases life in us. This life causes us to take actions that are courageous and full of faith. When we step out to serve God boldly, something is released in Heaven. When we move past worldly thoughts and trust in Him, supernatural things happen.

All faith needs an action

Just like Joshua, we are called to be very bold and very courageous. In Hebrews 10:38 the Lord tells us, “But my righteous one will live by faith. And I take no pleasure in the one who shrinks back.” This means that God takes great pleasure when we boldly step into what He has promised us. All faith needs an action. We know from the book of James that we prove our faith by the actions we take. As believers, we do not shrink back, for this does not please the Lord.

The Bible does not encourage us to grow in boldness and courage, we are simply commanded to be bold and courageous. God would not command us to do something if it was not within our new nature to do so. Your new nature in Christ has the ability to be supernaturally bold and courageous. It is part of who you really are.

When we think God's thoughts, faith wells up inside our hearts. Once we take action, life is released to us. This may happen in tiny ways or in very large ways. This happens in every day life. While parenting a child, while negotiating a business deal, while caring for an aged parent, while helping a neighbor, while serving at church, while praying for the sick. All of these are natural opportunities for the supernatural. Our spiritual thinking enables us to see that all good gifts come from our Father above (James 1:7).

Seeing what God sees

When we have the mind of Christ and begin to grow in our spiritual thinking, we begin to see the world like God sees it - through His eyes. When we see what God sees, it compels us to take actions that please Him. Our perspective is permanently changed when we see the world this way.

A man struggling with pornography dramatically changes his perspective once he realizes this is a very poor and low view of women. His heart is changed when he realizes he is a defender not a user of women, that women engaged in pornography are vulnerable people who need the Lord's love and compassion. His supernatural ability to see them through Christ's eyes has changed him permanently. Instead of using their vulnerability for his own selfish pleasure, his view of women changes, and his behavior changes automatically.

Transforming your narrative

You get to choose between two narratives to interpret the facts of your life. Life happens - the good and the bad. How you view these events is an indication of your level of spiritual thinking.

A friend of mine (whom I will call Bill to protect his identity) went for a series of medical procedures. After the tests his specialty physician confirmed that he had a terminal sickness. You can imagine how devastating the news was. We prayed together for God's healing power to be released in his body. We prayed for a miracle. A few weeks later Bill went to a second specialist who could find no traces of the illness. I was so excited and thanking God for the miracle. Bill, however, started having doubts. He wondered if the first physician had simply made a mistake. All the facts that relate to this entire story could be interpreted in a worldly way or in a spiritual way. It seemed to me that the probability of the first physician making such a great mistake, given the variety of tests and procedures he had performed, was extremely low. Bill was not so sure. By the way, Bill is a believer. Bill had a choice to make: choose a world narrative or a spiritual narrative. He could interpret the facts in a worldly way and believe that the first physician made a mistake and that fortunately he had discovered the second physician who figured out that he was not sick at all; or, believe that God had healed him after his visit to the first physician and that the second physician confirmed the healing. I'm glad to report that Bill chose the latter.

Bill is not alone in this problem. I think a vast majority of Christians would be tempted to choose a worldly explanation. My son received a large tax bill for his business involving tens of thousands of dollars. He sought help from his CPA and it seemed there was absolutely nothing that could be done. He and his wife prayed for God's favor and supernatural intervention. A few days later, he received a phone call stating that he owed less than $100. They chose to interpret the facts in a heavenly way and thank God for His supernatural blessing. No doubt,

God used several key people to make that happen but it was not the key people that made it happen - it was God. Remember, **all** good gifts come from the Father no matter who He uses to accomplish it.

The Holy Spirit would love to help you interpret the events of your life from His perspective. He would love to show you how to think about these events. Perhaps it has never occurred to you to ask the Lord to show you how He thinks about these events. Perhaps some of the events are so painful that you do not wish to think about them. Jesus desires to bring healing and wholeness into every area of your life. He wants to heal your heart so that you think and feel freely. This can only happen when you come to Jesus and ask Him to show you how you are to think about these definitive events.

Actions change emotions

Have you ever noticed that your emotions are subject to action? Perhaps you are feeling discouraged and decide to take a walk. The walk seems to change your mood. If you are feeling self-pity and decide to do something for someone else, self-pity evaporates and you feel good. Let's take another look at our diagram and add the next piece for discussion (see diagram on next page).

Let's make this very simple. Your heart is wired to: think, decide, feel.

It is important to understand that actions do not have to be substantial in order for emotions to be affected. Even small actions can have tangible effects on your emotions. If I'm discouraged and I raise my hands towards Heaven in worship, my emotions begin to change. As I continue to sing a song of praise, my mood changes. If I shout praises to the Lord, joy begins to fill my heart. Simple actions can cause big mood changes.

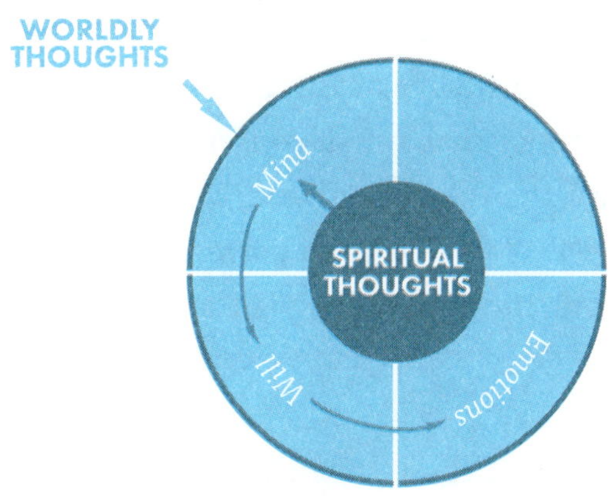

The combination of life-giving thoughts and actions is a powerful means to manage your mood. I wish I had more time to explain the intricacies of how this works but it is beyond the scope of this book. Suffice it to say, God means for you to have a heart that is turned to Him and filled with His love, His peace, and His joy. He does not intend for you to be a victim of difficult circumstances, harsh environments and worldly people. You may find yourself in these type of conditions externally, but internally you can enjoy His peace that passes all understanding. Your outer world does not determine your inner world. The exact opposite is true.

Completing the circle

As we complete our diagram, we see that healthy emotions help us enjoy a clear conscience.

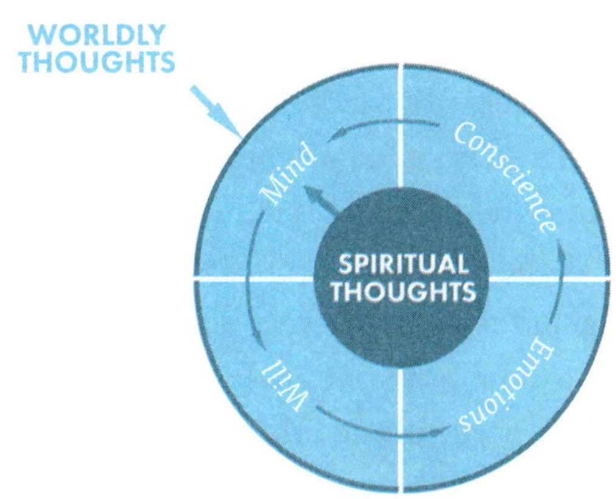

In previous chapters we discussed the fact that Jesus is the one who cleanses our conscience and we live lives free of condemnation. As we complete the circle, we notice that a clear conscience encourages godly thoughts. Now you have the full cycle that drives the internal energy and power of the believer. You have been powerfully and wonderfully made. The cycle in your heart was designed to bring you into total freedom in Christ.

This concludes our discussion about the heart and how it works. Over the last few chapters we have learned how toxic thoughts lead to poor decisions, toxic emotions, and a poor conscience, and that this negative process physically creates toxicity in every cell in our body.

We discussed how we have been given the mind of Christ that wields incredible power to take negative thoughts captive and release the life-giving thoughts that flow from our inner being - from the Lord. We showed how faith needs an action and how actions can affect our emotions positively. All this leads to a clear conscience and a freer mind.

We said it all starts with the process of renewing our minds. It is like downloading an app to your smart phone and then receiving daily updates. These updates add new features and new capabilities. God is constantly offering you upgrades to walk in all the fullness of the life He has for you.

It's very important for you begin to think in a spiritual way and not a worldly way, to translate the facts and events of your life with a heavenly narrative and not a worldly one. As you begin to believe in the finished work of the cross, life will be released in your heart. You will find the life of God transforming and redeeming every area of your life. As the fountain of life begins to flow from within, you'll discover that your transformation is effortless, peaceful and full of joy.

In the next chapter we're going to explore the practical aspects of the human spirit. We will discuss the incredible capabilities that the human spirit possesses and how God uses those capabilities to release His love and life in our hearts.

23

CHAPTER TWENTY THREE

THE FUNCTIONS OF THE HUMAN SPIRIT

We have finally reached my favorite topic in this entire book. Together, we will discover how God has wired you for a relationship with Him. He has built into your human spirit divine capabilities that make you more than human. You have been made in God's own image and that means you have certain God-like capabilities that enable you to relate to an Eternal being - God himself.

We're going to discuss the three core functions of the human spirit: the supernatural ability to **receive** from God, **relate** to that which you have received, and supernaturally **respond** in a way that transforms your life and those around you.

You have these three capabilities:

- the supernatural ability to **receive** spiritual things in the spiritual realm
- the supernatural ability to **relate** and connect with that which you received from Heaven
- the supernatural ability to **respond** to God, yourself, and others which transforms you and the world around you.

Here is a simple diagram to help you visualize this truth:

Making it simple

The simplest way to understand this is that God wants you to:

- Get it!
- Connect with it!
- Be it!

Our spiritual lives become dry when we try to use our weaker capabilities (like our mind, emotions, or will) as the primary means to be spiritual. We have discussed at length that God means for His life to flow through your human spirit, into your heart to transform you, and then into your soul to define you. He is not asking you to create human imitations of spiritual realities. You don't have to mimic and try to copy what you see in Scripture. You need to receive all that God has given you through the finished work of the cross, and then connect with that in a way that changes your thinking and transforms your life. At that point, change happens effortlessly as the life of God flows out of your spirit and into your heart. All transformation occurs in a state in which you rest in the finished work of the cross. Because you've now been transformed by the life of God within you, you discover your new self and act accordingly.

Your mind does not have the capability to receive in the same way that your spirit does. Think about it for a minute. If someone is having an encounter with God and enjoying the overwhelming sense of His presence and love, there is an emotional reaction to that. However, the emotional reaction is fully under their control, even if they don't care to control it, because they are enjoying His presence so much. Nonetheless, there is a human reaction to a spiritual event. This is where many believers are confused. They believe that God may overwhelm their emotions and force them to do things they don't want to do.

Now that you understand how you're wired, you can see that a spiritual event occurs in your spirit and overflows into your emotions and your mind.

You are wired like God is wired

Because you have been given powerful capabilities in God, He expects you to use them, enjoy them and live in them. Life in the Spirit is about learning to use these capabilities as a way of life. These are not tools that you reach for when you need something from God. These capabilities are the inherent attributes of who you are as a new creation being. You are a participant in His divine nature and therefore share the same attributes with Him.

The supernatural ability to receive

This part of the book helps you put it all together. Now you can understand why we've been saying that the Kingdom of God is received and not achieved. We can state in clear terms what we mean by this. The Kingdom of God is received in a spiritual way and not in an intellectual way. Now it may make more sense why your spirit has far more capability than your mind. Your capacity to receive is a 1,000 times larger than your ability to think. Your spirit can receive instant revelation from God and immediately get it. It may take your mind years to be transformed and renewed by this revelation. This is the key to spiritual growth. If you make your mind the main thing you will grow very slowly, but if you teach your mind to be submitted to the truth in your spirit, you will enjoy a rapid spiritual growth. As the life of God flows through you, His love and revelation will transform your thinking. You will find that you "know that you know" without your mind being fully able to explain why or how you know. Each time you try to explain it your mind will understand more and more until it catches up with what your spirit understands.

Perhaps it'll be clearer to you now why unbelief is the primary sin under the new covenant because unbelief stops you from receiving. Unbelief is nothing more than choosing to ignore your spiritual ability to receive. God wants you to receive His grace, His gift of righteousness, and your inheritance in Christ. The only way for this to happen is for you to exercise your supernatural ability to receive from God. If your mind is the primary gateway for what you believe, you will believe very little.

Remember, at the core of the heart is the spirit. We are talking about the capabilities of the spirit. Your human spirit enables the outer functions of your heart to function correctly - your mind, will, emotions, and conscience. For the outer functions of your heart to be transformed and constantly invigorated by the life of God, you have to learn to use your spirit-receiver. It is an act of faith.

Keeping your spirit-receiver on

I love movies. For me, the best part is being immersed in a different reality for 2 hours. Nothing destroys that immersion experience faster than someone who interrupts the movie or talks through it. The unnecessary talking creates a strange scenario where the current reality is blended with the reality the movie producer is trying to create.

An abundant life is only possible if you learn to have your spirit-receiver *on* and *downloading*. Interruptions interfere with that spiritual reality. What is different from the movie analogy is that you are designed to live in both realities simultaneously - the heavenly realm and the earthly realm. You are seated with Him in Heavenly places and you live in your natural world.

God made you with the dual capability. When believers do not use their spiritual capabilities, they remain worldly and never learn the power of God's world interfacing with the natural world.

It is not blind faith

The Kingdom of God is not about blind faith for narrow-minded and uneducated people. If intelligence and education were the sole means of spirituality, the smartest people would be the most spiritual and that is certainly not true. The Kingdom of God is about people who exercise their supernatural capability to receive from God - all that He purchased on the cross for them.

The ability to believe God and receive all that He has done for you, is a supernatural ability that has been given to every human being. Otherwise, the Bible would be misleading by telling us that it is God's will that all men be saved. It says in 1 Timothy 2:3-4 , "This is good, and pleases God our Savior, who wants all people to be saved and to come to a knowledge of the truth."

When you say, "I cannot believe that", what you are really saying is, "I am choosing to not use my spiritual capability to receive." I doubt that anybody has intentionally chosen not to use the spiritual capability in this way, but that is the effect. In the next chapter we will discuss this capability in much more detail.

The supernatural power to connect with God and His truth

The second supernatural capability that God has given you is the capacity to connect with Him and with His truth. It is the capacity to

relate. Once you've received His grace and the revelation of His love for you, you have a supernatural capability to connect with that truth and <u>make it real for you</u>. This capability ignites the outer functions of your heart (mind, will, emotions, and conscience) and enables you to understand and be transformed by what you've received.

Built into this capability is an authority from God to release power into your life. Your mind becomes renewed and your emotions become reenergized when you exercise this supernatural faculty.

God commanded you to renew your mind. It would be unfair and even ridiculous for Him to ask you to do this if you had no supernatural capability to do so! It would be the same as telling someone to forget their culture. The mind cannot renew itself. This in the natural is like trying to pull yourself up by pulling on your shoelaces. Most people have already tried to change by self effort. The mind, by itself, can only explore different ideas and thoughts and choose between them. Your supernatural capability goes far deeper than that. It enables you to transform your thinking in a very deep way.

Ephesians 4 tells you to be renewed in the <u>*spirit*</u> of your mind. Now you understand what the Scripture means by this. The Scripture is not asking you to just think different thoughts. It is commanding you to transform the deep thinking of your mind. We know from earlier chapters that the deep thoughts of God flow through your spirit into your mind (dianoia). It is this supernatural capability that allows you to "repent" and transform your thinking radically - in an instant. Transformation is not a long process. We have all had that moment when we truly "get it" and "connect with it" and we are changed. At that point we are not the same person we were a few minutes earlier. A transformation took place.

Without this capability being exercised, all you can do is slowly evolve your thinking as you are exposed to new information. Your supernatural ability to relate to what God has given you supersedes information and enables transformation. This is the ability to take God's truth and make it yours. It is the ability to relate to Him as you would a Father. It is the ability to see yourself as a bride and as a son. It is what enables you to receive His love for you and be transformed by it.

It moves what you have received in your spirit and pushes it into every aspect of your life. It transforms your thinking, it empowers your purpose (will) and ignites your emotions with supernatural feelings. This capability keeps your conscience clear.

Your supernatural ability to relate, makes your relationship with God very real! This is the ability to connect with God and with His truth. With this ability, you have the authority to be free in Jesus and see every aspect of your life redeemed. It is this ability that enables you to enjoy intimacy with God.

It is this ability that transforms your definition of your self. It is this understanding that allows you to upgrade your thinking about who you are and about who God is for you.

The supernatural ability to respond

Once you've received what God has supernaturally given you and you've connected with it using your supernatural ability to relate to it, you get to respond in a way that transforms who you are and blesses those around you.

This capability supernaturally empowers you to respond to God in worship and adoration. When you get what He has done for you and it has become real to you, you find yourself automatically responding to God with a heart of gratitude and praise. You suddenly get that you have been forgiven and been given a grand inheritance in the Kingdom.

You respond in thanksgiving and worship to your heavenly Father who loves you. You find yourself worshiping from a very deep place. This is a deeply satisfying and enjoyable type of worship. That is why we are commanded to worship Him in *spirit* and in *truth*.

This is the heart of the believer's walking in step with the Spirit. This is the being and the doing part. This supernatural capability allows you to respond in a spiritual way and not in a worldly way. It allows you to respond to God in a spiritual way, respond to yourself in a spiritual way, and respond to others in a spiritual way.

It is this ability that enables you to "reign in life" and walk by the Spirit as God intended. This is so exciting and empowering that it transforms and transcends everything you believed you were capable of enjoying in God. When you respond using this faculty, you will hardly recognize yourself. To put it more accurately, you will recognize your true self in Christ and see who you really are. It is from this place that you can resist the devil and see him flee (James 4:7). It is from this place that you can rule and govern your life in step with the Holy Spirit. It is from this place that you can see the lives of others being restored and supernaturally transformed. It is from this place that spiritual ministry occurs.

We will spend some time in a later chapter discussing this capability in more detail.

Spiritual functioning versus worldly functioning

When you walk in the Spirit, you are functioning in the three capabilities that we've just discussed. You are able to receive from God, connect with what you have received and make it real to you. You then act on it and become that which you've received. The Scriptures will begin to make a lot more sense when you read them from a spiritual point of view. So, when the Bible says "put off the old man" and "put on the new man", it means "use your spiritual capability to perform this task". If you were to read those Scriptures in a worldly way, you would be confused by what they mean. Perhaps you would be tempted to try to mimic spiritual behavior and attributes through your own self effort.

Unfortunately, many believers are caught in this terrible trap.

The worldly trap

It is a great sadness to see how worldly thinking is so prevalent in the body of Christ. Whether it is intellectualism, emotionalism, self-help (self effort driven by human will), or simple unbelief - it is all worldliness. God has offered us so much more. He has offered us a life in step with the Spirit that releases His life through us to the world around us. God did not leave supernatural living to our own human strength. He did not intend for us to imitate spiritual behaviors. He wants us to learn how to enable His life to flow through us. He has given us powerful capabilities. He has built into our human spirit the ability for the life of God to flow abundantly through us.

The empowered life

God went to extraordinary lengths to reach out and pluck you from your depraved world of sin and place you in Christ. You are now seated with Him in heavenly places, which means that heavenly capabilities are now ignited in you to empower you to live the life He intended for you. It is a life of wonder and power. The more you get to know Jesus, the more His grace flows through you. You can receive the Kingdom, see your life transformed by it, and step out bringing Heaven to Earth!

At this stage of the book we are pulling all the elements together which hopefully makes more sense to you. We started our discussion by understanding how God has wired us. We then discussed His grace and the transformative power of the new covenant. And now we are discussing how we live this.

Once again, we are fascinated with the Lord's kindness to us. Not only did Jesus bring us life through His sacrifice on the cross, but God also has given us supernatural ability to relate to Him. He has given each person the ability to receive grace and truth. He has empowered every person to connect and be changed by that truth.

He is redefining who you are so that you can discover your true nature in Christ.

God wants you to get it, connect with it, and be it. He wants you to believe it, let it change you, and walk in it.

24

CHAPTER TWENTY FOUR

THE SUPERNATURAL ABILITY TO RECEIVE

It is the supernatural ability to receive that enables us to receive Christ. It creates a level playing field for every person on Earth. Everybody can receive Christ. It is this essential capability that makes it reasonable for God to say that it is His will that all men be saved. If you are sharing the gospel with somebody who has a mind that is completely opposed to the message of Christ, they have the ability to believe and bypass all the years of wrong thinking. Regardless of religious background, ethnic upbringing, ignorance, and anti-Christian thought, every person has been given the supernatural ability to accept Christ if they choose to exercise this faculty. "Yet to all who did receive him, to those who believed in his name, he gave the right to become children of God--" (John 1:12 NIV).

Paul makes it clear that everything we have, we have because we received it. In 1 Corinthians 4:7, he asks a provocative question: "For who makes you different from anyone else? What do you have that you did not receive? And if you did receive it, why do you boast as though you did not?" Everything in the Kingdom of God is received, including the Kingdom itself.

Receiving Christ initiates everything

The day you receive Christ you receive everything that Christ purchased on your behalf. On that day you are fully qualified to receive everything from Heaven as your inheritance "...how much more will those who **receive** God's abundant provision of grace and of the gift of righteousness reign in life through the one man, Jesus Christ!" (Romans 5:17).

Jesus is the way, the truth, and the life. When you receive Him, you receive the way, the truth, and the life. Here are some of the other things you receive when you receive Christ:

- You receive **forgiveness** for sin once and for all
- You receive a **new nature** which makes you a participant of His divine nature
- You receive **the gift of righteousness**
- You receive a **cleansed conscience**
- You receive a **purpose** from Heaven for your life
- You receive the **favor** of God on your life
- You receive **abundant grace**
- You receive a new **position** - seated with Christ
- You receive **freedom from the law**
- You receive **freedom from the power of sin**
- You receive **freedom from worldliness**
- You receive **healing**
- You receive the **love of the Father**
- You receive the **fellowship of the Holy Spirit**
- You receive a **new Lord** of your life - Jesus
- You receive new **authority** to live the life for which Jesus paid

You received all these things and more. These were not things that you developed in your life or things for which you worked. Everything in the Kingdom is by faith from first to last. Faith is the expression of your faculty to receive, and the faculty of your human spirit that enables you to hope for spiritual things and expect good things from God. Remember what the Bible says in Hebrews 11:1 NIV, "Now faith is **confidence** in what we <u>hope</u> for and **assurance** about what we do not see."

The Christian life is about learning to walk in that which we have freely received. Perhaps now the instructions of the New Testament make more sense to you. The reason that you're told to do something is because you yourself have been a recipient of that same thing. Everything you're commanded to do under the new covenant, you have been enabled to do. For example, when the Scriptures require you to forgive others it is because you have freely received God's forgiveness.

An easy way to think of this is to use a financial illustration. If I tell my son to give his sister $100, he has to make a difficult decision. He looks at his savings and sees that he has $120 saved. If he gives his sister $100, it dramatically depletes his resources and leaves him in a much poorer state. If, however, I give my son $1,000 and tell him to give his sister $100 he is in a very different position. Because he has freely received, it is very easy for him to freely give. He is not depleted but enriched by the process.

Because we have so freely received from Heaven, we are able to freely give without being depleted. This generosity of the Father's heart is expressed in every instruction given to us under the new covenant. When the Bible tells us to forgive, be hospitable, be patient, be generous, etc., it is telling us to express God's true nature. Since we participate in the divine nature, it is now our new normal to be generous on every occasion. It gets better. Not only did we receive everything from God freely, but we received it in great abundance. Have you ever noticed that the New Testament always speaks about our inheritance using superlatives? Here are a few extracts from Ephesians 1 to illustrate this,

"Praise be to the God... who has blessed us in the heavenly realms with **every spiritual blessing** in Christ. ... to the praise of his **glorious grace**, which he has **freely given us** in the One he loves. ... that he **lavished on us**. ... that you may know the hope to which he has called you, the riches of his **glorious inheritance** in his holy people, and his **incomparably great power for us** who believe."

God has put in writing that you have been blessed with every spiritual blessing in Christ. You have received His abundant grace which He has lavished on you so that you can understand His purpose for you. He has given you a glorious inheritance filled with incomparably great power. I want to drive home the point that this is not a theoretical or poetic description of your position in Christ. This is a very real and powerful description of who you are and what you have received in Christ. His grace towards you is more abundant than you will ever need. His willingness to give you more grace can only be described as lavish and unrestrained.

The inheritance that He has for you will make His purpose for your life and your relationship with Him seem glorious. The power you need to walk in all that He has for you is the same power that raised Jesus from the dead. It is a great and incomparable power. Please notice that I added nothing to that description. I simply used the same superlatives from the NIV translation.

When the mind reads something like the passage in Ephesians 1, it can only mentally ascend to the idea. It cannot believe it. Believing is a function reserved for the human spirit. God does not want us to give mental assent to the Scriptures. He wants us to believe the Scriptures. We can read the Scriptures in a worldly way and never mix it with faith. This is always the danger of intellectualized Christianity. It is devoid of power. This type of Christianity provides us enough of Jesus to get someone saved and nothing more. The Holy Spirit invites us to a far more lavish and glorious inheritance than simply understanding intellectual Christian concepts. This is why James 1:21 says, "... receive with meekness the implanted word, which is able to save your souls."

When we read the Bible, we engage our spirit-receiver to allow God's life to flow through us. The heart reaction is a secondary effect. Whatever the mind, will, emotions, and conscience react to is secondary to the primary event of receiving God's word. Spending time daily in God's word is way more exciting when you are engaged to receive God's love and life into your inner being. This is a 1,000 times more wonderful than reading the Bible intellectually.

Any truth we receive in this way transforms us. If we read the Scriptures in a merely intellectual way, we remain dry. Truth that does not transform leads to dry religion. Our objective is to increase the flow of the fountain. Remember our analogy from earlier in the book?

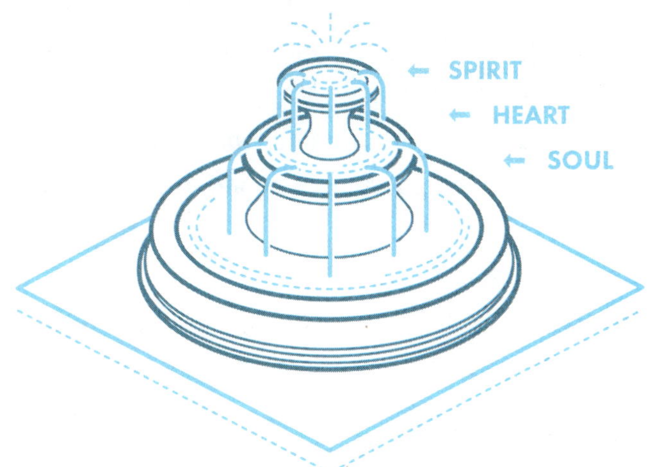

We need to read enough Scripture to cause the life of God to flow into every area of our hearts and to define us in our soul. Allow the Scriptures to define you. Remember these definitions are received not achieved. You don't have to behave like a son to be one. If one of my children misbehaves, their status as my child has not changed. Their behavior does not determine their definition. How much more true is this in our relationship with God the Father? When the Scriptures define you as "more than conqueror", it means for you to be defined that way.

The Holy Spirit is the author of the Scriptures. He intends to be part of the process when you receive the Scriptures. He wants to lead you into all truth. He wants to show you the way you need to go. He loves to talk to you about what the Scriptures mean for you. When you read the Scriptures, it is good to have a conversation with the Holy Spirit while you're reading. His job is to take the written words off the page and translate them into life for your soul. Jesus encouraged us to drink deeply of the Holy Spirit (John 7:37).

Imagine that you are visiting your friend who lives on a farm. During your visit, his barn catches fire. You rush out to extinguish the flames but the only thing you can find is a faucet with no hose attached. You cannot find a bucket so you begin taking scoops of water with your hands and throwing it at the fire. Your chance of success in this mode of operation is obviously very low. Many believers try to address the challenges of their lives by the little scoops of truth their minds can carry. God intends for you to enjoy a pipeline connected to heavens resources flowing through your life. It is possible to turn the pipeline off and revert back to handfuls of truth.

You have been fully qualified in Christ to receive what He has for you. More than that, He has provided you with a spiritual capability to receive everything He has for you. You can exercise this supernatural faculty to receive any time you like. It is up to you how much you receive from God. But know this, you have a glorious inheritance and incomparably great power available to you.

You can receive healing from past emotional wounds using this spiritual capacity. In the same way, you can receive physical healing for your body.

This is exactly what Peter did when he arrived at the gate beautiful and found the lame man sitting there begging for alms. Peter told him that he did not have silver and gold to give him but he would give him that which he had received from the Lord - healing! (Acts 3:6).

Perhaps it is time for you to set a few hours aside to receive from the Lord. You know now that He is very willing to lavish His grace on you. You know that you have the ability to perceive all that He has for you. You know that Jesus has fully qualified you to receive all that He purchased on your behalf. God has done all the work so that you can be the recipient of a glorious life. This is not to say that you will not have pain or difficulties in your life. This is to say that regardless of what life throws at you, you can receive all you need from the Lord to live in joy and peace. Your internal life is determined by what you choose to receive from God.

A rich inner life flowing with the life of God will cause you to become a blessing to others. Receiving from God not only transforms you, but also transforms your relationships. Soon you'll be the one receiving from Heaven on behalf of others. This is called intercession. This is why we pray for one another. This is why we lay hands on one another. This is why we bless one another.

The kingdom of Heaven has been designed to be received in such a simple way that a child can do it. This is why children are often more capable of receiving from God than adults. They have not yet learned to use their minds instead of the spirit. A child naturally receives. To intellectualize Christianity this may seem to be naïve. Once again this is a limited mental view of a spiritual reality.

The ability to recognize truth

Let's take a minute to explore the fact that you can receive revelation and truth. 1 John 2:27 says, "But the anointing which you have **received** from Him abides in you, and you do not need that anyone teach you; but as the **same anointing teaches you concerning all things**, and is true, and is not a lie, and just as it has taught you, you will abide in Him."

When God enables you to do something in a supernatural way, it is called an anointing. Another way to say this is: anointing is God's ability in you to enable you to do something with ease.

John tells us that we have received an anointing from Him that has the ability to teach us about all things.

Have you ever sat in a sermon or a lecture and felt that something was off? You could not put your finger on it but it did not sit right in your spirit. Your mind could not analyze the problem and your emotions could not detect it either. Something deeper in you told you that something was off. Perhaps you've had this experience when one of your children told you they were telling the truth but you knew it was a lie. You could not prove that it was a lie but you "knew that you knew."

The Holy Spirit uses this supernatural capability to teach you about all things. He may use a sermon, a movie, the Scriptures, a conversation with a friend, or a communication in your spirit. When this function is activated, you feel it. It is like something that jumps up in your heart and grabs the truth and says, "pay attention to this!" It seems to capture your attention, your imagination, and your heart all at the same time.

There is another interesting verse in 1 John 4:6, which says "We are of God. He who knows God hears us; He who is not of God does not hear us. **By this we know the spirit of truth and the spirit of error."**

The ability to see others as they really are

The same ability allows us to see people the way that Heaven sees them. It is a supernatural capability to see beyond somebody's behavior and personality and see who they are in Christ. That supernatural perception is empowered by the Holy Spirit. It is a mechanism of revelation. He reveals to you who people really are and this enables you to see them as He sees them. This empowers you to show them unconditional love. It produces a deep love for people and a patience with them.

The Lord's great kindness towards you has wired you to receive as much of Him as you desire. He has fully qualified you in Jesus to receive a glorious inheritance. He made sure that you have the supernatural capability to receive. He is truly the kindest person you'll ever meet.

25

CHAPTER TWENTY FIVE

THE SUPERNATURAL ABILITY TO RELATE

This supernatural ability is as exciting as the ability to receive. This is the ability that helps you connect with God and with His truth. It is the ability that makes the spiritual life real and active in our lives. Every human being has been given this supernatural capability built into their human spirit. Several times we've talked about the extraordinary idea that a being trapped in time and space can relate to a Being that is outside of time and space. It is mind blowing to think that a created human being has the capacity to relate to a timeless all-powerful Creator. What separates man from animal is a human spirit with the capacity to have relationship with an eternal God.

Of all the ways in which a relationship with an eternal Being could be made possible, God chose the most intimate version. He chose to make His home in us. Jesus said, "If anyone loves Me, he will keep My word; and My Father will love him, and **We will come to him and make Our home with him**" (John 14:23 NKJV). He chose to become one with us. He did not choose to provide us with a remote communication mechanism. He did not set up a social media mechanism in which He could post blogs and tweets. He moved in! He chose to hide us with

Christ in God. Wow! What an extraordinary way to build a permanent and eternal relationship. Colossians 3:3 says, "For you died, and your life is **hidden with Christ** in God."

This is a core truth to understand. Because you have become one with Him, your spirit has become alive to Him. Your supernatural faculty to relate enables you to make Him real to you and make His truth relevant to your life. You know that you can receive anything you need from God and that He has purchased everything for you. You know that you are fully qualified in Christ and wired by the Father to receive.

Your heavenly Father

The news gets even better. The Scripture shows that we have the ability given by God to relate to Him. We can connect with Him because He makes it possible. We can enjoy fellowship with God as our heavenly Father. Jesus made a big deal about this. He really wanted us to get the idea that God is a Father. More than that, He is **your** heavenly Father. He's a perfect Father that loves you perfectly and wants you to enjoy that relationship in a very deep and personal way. If your relationship with your earthly father has been marred in any way, He brings healing to your heart so that you can truly know Him as a Father.

To ensure that you come to know Him as a Father, God sent His Spirit to teach you how to relate to Him in this way. It is our friend, the Holy Spirit, who teaches us to relate to God - not as a servant relates to a master - but as a son/daughter relates to a Father. This is why we feel the need to call Him Father because the Holy Spirit intentionally works that in us. Look in Galatians 4:6 "And because you are **sons**, God has sent forth the Spirit of His Son into your hearts, crying out, "**Abba, Father!**""

Perhaps, you have seen yourself solely as the Lord's servant. He sees you as His son. God has male and female sons and He has a male and female bride. The reason God uses the word "sons" is to denote the idea that

His children receive an inheritance. In the cultural setting into which the Scriptures were written, only sons received an inheritance and the firstborn son was treated with priority. Under the new covenant we know that there is "neither male nor female" in Christ and that we are all coheirs. The truth Scripture is showing us here is that both male and female "sons" receive a firstborn inheritance from their heavenly Father. Women must get used to the idea of being spiritual sons in the same way that men must get used to the idea of being a spiritual bride. Each metaphor is a beautiful picture of who God is to us personally. The Holy Spirit works in us to respond to the Father as a son and to respond to Jesus as a bride.

The power to be transformed

Our interaction with God is always transformational. He is not trying to inform us about who He is, but He is transforming us to be like Him. We were made in His image and He is restoring and redeeming us back to our original design. All truth and all interactions with God are transformational.

We are able to transform our thinking. We previously discussed what the word "repent" really means. When you understand who the Lord is for you, you change your mind - take a different view and upgrade your thinking. Repentance is therefore a powerful means to connect with the truth of who God is and who you are in Him. Take a different view of who He is for you. Allow Him to inform you about your true identity. It is your spirit capability that enables you to connect with the revelation of who He is and who you are in Him. It is the power to be able to agree with such a revelation and to go with it. Fortunately, this power is not dependent on your theological training or education. It is about a deeper type of "knowing".

Your supernatural capability enables you to "realize" the truth - make it real. Jesus said, "On that day you will **realize** that I am in my Father, and you are in me, and I am in you" (John 14:20 NIV). That word "realize" means to have deep, personal and intimate knowledge. It means that you will know in the core of your being. The Greek word is ginṓskō, and Strong's definition says it means to "know (absolutely) in a great variety of applications and with many implications —to allow, be aware of, feel, have knowledge, perceived, be resolved, can speak, be sure, understand."

This ability to "know" is a supernatural capability that carries with it the authority to allow or disallow.

Parents are instructed to teach the children to **know** the Lord and not to **know about** the Lord. To know the Lord involves your entire being and to know about the Lord involves your mind. The Holy Spirit works in us so that we can **know the Lord** in a deep and personal way. Our supernatural faculty to relate allows us to **know the Lord** in this way and to move beyond just knowing facts about Him.

Remember the verse in Romans 2:4? It says, "Or do you show contempt for the riches of his kindness, forbearance and patience, not realizing that God's kindness is intended to lead you to repentance?" God's kindness helps us understand who He really is and to be able to relate to that in our own personal way.

The authority to "Let"

The Lord has given you the authority to agree with Heaven. His word in your mouth has the same power as His word in His mouth when we are aligned with Him. We discussed previously the idea that we can "let" spiritual truths reign in our lives.

Here is a sample of the things we have authority to "let" in our lives:

- Let your gentleness be evident to all. (Philippians 4:5 NIV)
- Let the peace of Christ rule in your hearts. (Colossians 3:15 NIV)

- Let the message of Christ dwell among you richly.(Colossians 3:16 NIV)
- Let your conversation be always full of grace. (Colossians 4:6 NIV)
- Let nothing move you. (1 Corinthians 15:58 NIV)
- Let perseverance finish its work so that you may be mature and complete, not lacking anything. (James 1:4 NIV)

Here are some "Do not let's":

- Do not let anyone deceive you in any way. (2 Thessalonians 2:3 NIV)
- Do not let anyone look down on you because you are young. (1 Timothy 4:12 NIV)
- Do not let anyone despise you. (Titus 2:15 NIV)
- Do not let it trouble you. (1 Corinthians 7:21 NIV)
- Do not let yourselves be burdened again by a yoke of slavery (the law). (Galatians 5:1 NIV)
- Do not let the sun go down while you are still angry, (Ephesians 4:26 NIV)

You have spiritual authority in your life to allow and disallow things in your life. This power is part of the incomparably great power given to you in Christ. You can simply **let** the peace of Christ reign in your life. Like a parcel being delivered to your door, you can choose to sign for it or not sign for it. You can authorize what you receive and what you do not receive. You do not have to sign for every package that arrives at your door simply because it arrived. When the enemy attempts to deliver a package that is not meant for you, he hopes you will sign for it and authorize it in your life. The Bible tells us clearly that all good gifts come from our heavenly Father. All the gifts He sends we should sign for and everything else we should refuse to sign for it.

To illustrate this let me share a story. A man in our congregation came to me and said, "My wife and children do not respect me spiritually." I know the man and I told him that I was not surprised that this was the case. My response surprised him. I explained, "You know that as the head of your family you have the authority to allow and disallow spiritual realities in your home. If you are passive then whatever spiritual reality exists in your home is allowed. If however, you actively decide in prayer what is allowed and disallowed you can change the spiritual atmosphere of your home. I happen to know from the things you have shared with me that you have no regard for spiritual authority. You do not respect any spiritual authority in your life and therefore a disregard for spiritual authority is allowed in your home. Your wife and children are simply being mirrors - they are reflecting the spiritual reality you have allowed. You can change this through prayer by disallowing that spirit and by demonstrating your own submission to spiritual authority. When your family sees you submitting to Jesus - who is the true head of your home - a different reality and atmosphere will be authorized in your home."

He was surprised by the idea that he had this type of spiritual capability. He had never heard this before. He is a good man with a good heart but was simply unaware of the authority that he had to allow and disallow in the spiritual realm.

God is not calling men to be mini dictators in their home and to dominate their family. This is not His way. His way is a life of submission in the same way that Jesus submitted to His Father which empowered Him to do all God had called Him to do. Submission is a believer thing. Jesus is in submission to His Father. The church is in submission to Jesus. Husbands are in submission to Christ. Wives are in submission to their husbands. Children are in submission to their parents. This is not a hierarchy. This is a mechanism for release and empowerment. While it is not the scope of this book to deal with the imbalances of certain Christian teachings about the structure of the biblical home, suffice it to say that God always calls us to a place that sets us free. Freedom does not mean a lack of accountability. God calls us to a place of security and freedom through our relationships. Husbands are meant to create wide spaces for their wives and children. They are to be their greatest fans and lay down their lives for them. A wife should feel the same way the church does - "my boundaries have fallen in pleasant places and oh how he loves me!"

The power to rest

Previously we discussed the very powerful idea that God wants us to live a worry free life with no anxiety. He provided a way for us to deal with all our negative thoughts spiritually to free our minds to think positive thoughts. As we have come to expect from the Lord, it gets even better. The more you grow in Christ, you'll discover it keeps getting better and better. You may think that the gospel of grace is truly wonderful, but dig a little and you'll find there is so much more.

Not only does God want us to live a worry free life, He wants us to live from a place of rest. Because you have the supernatural capability to relate, you have the power to trust the Lord whom you love. When you trust someone, you're able to leave a matter in their hands. If you believe that somebody is capable and competent you are more likely to leave it to them to take care of it for you. Your ability to supernaturally connect with the Lord enables you to fully trust Him with every detail of your life. This frees your mind to focus on things that are true, noble, right, pure, lovely, admirable, excellent, or praiseworthy (Philippians 4:8 NIV). It also enables you to find rest for your soul.

Hebrews 4:10 Tells us, "For anyone who **enters God's rest** also <u>rests from their works</u>, just as God did from his." You have the power from Heaven to enter and remain in God's rest. You no longer have to rely on your own works to be right with God. You are now at peace with God because of Jesus Christ. You can cease from your own self-righteous works. You can cease from worldliness that comes from not trusting God. Many of us are praying for God to answer our prayers so that we do not have to trust Him again. We pray that the Lord would help our business be successful so that we can be financially independent. That is a great prayer unless it comes from a worldliness that wants to be free from the need to trust God. When we enter God's rest we enter a place of peace and confidence in who He is. You can be in rest while in the middle of a crisis. When you came to Christ you entered God's rest. Just stay there. There is no need to leave.

You have the supernatural power to make spiritual truths a personal reality. You do not have to wait for your mind to understand it, your emotions to feel it, your will to want it, or your conscience to give you permission. Because you are in Christ, you are fully qualified to wield this power to allow spiritual truth to be fully manifested in your life. You can now grow very rapidly in the Lord. You do not have to settle for slow spiritual growth. You have been given a divine capability to release the truth of God's word in your life and enjoy all of its benefits. You have been given a heavenly faculty to enjoy God as your Father and to experience the wonder of Jesus as your Bridegroom!

26

CHAPTER TWENTY SIX

THE SUPERNATURAL ABILITY TO RESPOND

We have discovered so far that God has given us a supernatural ability to receive and to relate. Now we are going to look at the extraordinary capability that He has given us to respond. This supernatural faculty that enables us to respond to God goes beyond our natural capabilities. For us to really enjoy who the Lord is, to enjoy His love, and to walk in all that He has for us, it takes supernatural power and an endowment from Heaven.

When we came to Christ and received Him, we received new life. The book of John says that Jesus has life in Him and that He is life. Your life truly began the day you came to Jesus because life entered your being. You received Him, you relate to Him, and now you discover that you can respond to Him in a supernatural way.

Romans 4:6 tells us that we can live a new life. Our old man is dead and gone, we have become new creation beings. You have become a new creation in that God has removed from you all the definitions of your past and replaced them with His definition of you.

This powerful ability enables us to ask the Lord how to respond to others. We can ask the Lord how He wants us to respond to difficult people, a harsh email, a false accusation, or new opportunity. Open your heart to the Lord and from your inner being receive the answer to the question, "How should I respond to this situation Lord?" In this question you are using all three of your spirit-functions: you are receiving His wisdom, connecting with His wisdom (relating) and responding to His wisdom in a way that goes beyond your human abilities.

Rejoice

When Philippians 4 tells us that we need to rejoice in the Lord always, it is showing us that we have a supernatural capability to respond to God with a permanent heart of rejoicing. This function of your human spirit, when ignited by the life of God, causes you to rejoice. Joy does not come out of our relationship with circumstances but out of our relationship with Jesus. Joy is released in our lives when we understand who He is to us and for us.

Worship

The supernatural ability from God to respond gives you the ability to respond to the Lord, yourself and others in a supernatural way. Now that you belong to Christ you have a priestly capability. You are able to minister to the Lord and to worship Him. It is your new nature to love worship. It is your new nature to want to minister to the Lord and adore Him. It is your new nature to want to make His name glorious.

Standing in church on a Sunday morning, you may not feel emotionally like worshiping. Your mind might be racing with the challenges of your week. You may not feel like worshipping but your spirit can supersede all of that and worship God anyway. You have divine power to engage in worship regardless of what you're thinking, feeling or wishing to do. You can supersede the lesser functions of your heart (mind, will, and conscience) and worship God from a place of liberty and freedom. That's why we're called to worship Him in **spirit and in truth**. We're not called to give Him intellectual worship and emotional worship as much as we're called to worship Him from our inner being - from our human spirit. God has set us up as worshippers in our inner being. Whether we like the music or not, it does not matter. Our ability to worship is not dependent on a worship leader, the atmosphere, or the state of the lesser functions of our heart. Our ability to worship is a God-given capability that He has divinely empowered us with!

You are a priest. You have this divine faculty to initiate thanksgiving, praise and worship of your King. Your Lord and Savior wishes you to minister in this way because, as you minister to Him, He ministers to you. The Lord does not need your worship. He requires it because of what it produces in you. He asks you to be a worshipper because it helps you discover more of Him and releases your true nature in Christ when you do. When you respond to the Holy Spirit in this way you are walking in step with Him. As the Holy Spirit sets out to lead you into all truth about God's love and inheritance for you, He requires you to learn to be a worshipper. As you reach out to God and focus on who He is, you also release who you are in Him. This is why praising God in the midst of difficult circumstances completely transforms your state of being. It changes your emotional and mental state to receive more grace from Him. God has empowered you as a worshipper. Worship Him with abandon and give Him the glory due to His name.

Rule

Proverbs 16:32 tells us that, "he who rules his own spirit is more powerful than he who takes a city." I remember the Gulf War and the extraordinary job the American generals did in taking city after city. During those early days of that conflict, every city taken was met with praise and rejoicing. The media spent much time helping us understand the competence of the generals who led that initiative. The Bible says that if you are able to rule your own spirit you are greater than a general who takes a city!

Once again we see that God never commands us to do something that He hasn't given us the capability to do. You are well able to rule your own spirit. His supernatural power to rule has been given to you to rule your own heart. You are not a victim or subjected to other powers and forces that may rule over you. In fact, Scripture makes it very clear that you are called to reign in life - beginning with your inner world. Look at this verse in Romans 5:17, "For if by the one man's offense death reigned through the one, much more those who receive abundance of grace and of the gift of righteousness **will reign in life through the One, Jesus Christ.**" All great leaders and rulers learn to do so at their home base. In the same way, you have to learn to rule your own spirit before you're able to bring the Kingdom of God to others. There is direct correlation between your ability to rule your spirit and your ability to bring the Kingdom to others. Deep within your own spirit, the life of God flows into your heart and empowers your will. You find yourself having supernatural will-power. This is the manifestation of God's divine power enabling your life. When the Scripture tells us to let perseverance do its work in us, it is telling us to use our supernatural capability to rule our spirit.

Resist

James 4:7 tells us about another aspect of our supernatural capability when it says, "Therefore submit to God. **Resist** the devil and he will flee from you." This ability to resist is a supernatural capability that goes far beyond will-power. This is why James tells us that when we are walking in step with God, when we are submitted to Him, His life flows through us and empowers us to resist the devil. This capability can resist his plans in our personal lives as well as his plans in our communities and in our nation. We are called to push back the forces of hell and darkness as we step into authority in Christ and resist the enemy. This ability to respond to God in submission, empowers us to take authority over the things that are not of God in our lives and to push them back - resist them. How kind is the Lord that He would give us such an ability? He empowered you to never be a victim but to always be a victor! You are not subject to the power of sin and death since Christ broke that power over your life at the cross. This ability to resist evil is a profound strength, empowered by Heaven itself, to break the bondages that the enemy has put on your life. It is an authority from Heaven to restore what has previously been destroyed.

Restore

The Bible talks about the authority that God releases in Christ to restore inheritances that have been lost. Since you are in Christ, you have been given the same authority to restore that which the enemy has destroyed. Look at Isaiah 49:8, "In the time of my favor I will answer you, and in the day of salvation I will help you; I will keep you and will make you to be a covenant for the people, **to restore the land and to reassign its desolate inheritances."**

The modern-day church is impoverished. The enemy has found a way to make people afraid of the ministry and person of the Holy Spirit. Intellectualized Christianity and externalized religion have held people in bondage. We are not to sit in judgment over such people but to walk in compassion for them. It is time to see people set free and be restored to their inheritance in Christ. You have been given the divine power and authority from Heaven to restore God's inheritance in your life and in others. Part of your supernatural faculty to respond in authority and power, is the authority to restore. It is now up to us to call "Restore! Restore!"

We are called to restore all those places that have been decimated and left desolate. When we bring the Kingdom of God into people's lives and into our communities, transformation and restoration automatically take place. Jesus is life. And where He is Lord, (the Kingdom of God) life is released and restoration is the automatic result. We are called to take up the mantle of restoring our lives, our families, our communities, and our nation. With every calling God gives us, He gives us divine power to execute that calling. It is His supernatural capacity to be able to respond spiritually that enables us to go beyond our personalities and to behave with an authority that does not come from our own minds but with an authority that comes from Heaven. This is not natural. This is supernatural!

Isaiah 61:4 says, "They will **rebuild the ancient ruins** and **restore the places long devastated**; they will **renew the ruined cities** that have been devastated for generations." This verse touches us deeply in our spirit and ignites a passion from God. Oh Lord, that we would rebuild the ancient ruins, that we would restore the places long devastated, and that we would renew the ruined cities. So much of the gospel of grace lies in ruins because of externalized religion. The inheritance of the Bride of Christ has long laid devastated. It is time for Bible-believing, Spirit-empowered believers full of faith to rise up and claim these desolate places. It is time for us to rebuild the Bride's inheritance and to restore her to be as glorious as God intended. Jesus is returning for a glorious Bride who is walking in the fullness of who she is in Christ and enjoying her glorious inheritance in Him.

During my teenage years, my father decided to restore his very first car - a 1936 Morris Minor. He paid $36 for it when he was a teenager. He and I spent countless hours restoring that old car. Some of the doors were rusted through. The engine had to be rebuilt from the ground up. We had to rewire the car and build a new interior. He bought a second donor car to help us source additional parts. Fortunately, we lived on a small farm at the time and we had the space for such a project. But the garage looked like a war zone with parts everywhere. There were rusted and broken pieces everywhere you looked. If someone had come to visit us during this restoration period, they would have thought that we were fighting a lost cause. It was a complete mess. They would have believed there was no point in continuing such a project. Let me tell you, the day the project was completed was fantastic! We were so proud of that car. It was beautiful like the day it rolled off the production line. It had been lovingly restored back to its original condition.

Sometimes we may become discouraged when we see the state of the church worldwide. There is so much worldliness, unbelief, and inheritance that lies in desolation and ruin. When we read the Scriptures and see what God has called us to do, then look at the church, we become disillusioned. In the natural realm it may seem a hopeless cause. But we are called to respond to God in a supernatural way in order to restore His Bride to her glorious beauty. We go beyond what we see in the natural and walk in step with the Spirit to see her rebuilt, reestablished and re-empowered. The church is the hope of the world. It is not governments, education, nonprofit organizations, it is the church of Jesus Christ, because the church hosts the very life of Heaven - Jesus Christ himself. With Jesus as her head she is able to bring life and transform her communities and see cities restored and rebuilt. It is time for the church to rise up to be the beautiful Bride the bridegroom expects. When Jesus returns, He is returning for a glorious Bride!

There are many parts of the body of Christ today that are entangled with externalized religion and intellectualized Christianity. They are parts devoid of power and have created a theology of powerlessness to support their modus operandi. When we talk about the church being the solution to the world's problems, we are aligning ourselves with Heaven's plan for mankind. Because of the church, there should be no injustice in this world. The church has the authority and power from Heaven to address every social evil and challenge. The church is Jesus's body to show compassion and love to a broken and needy world. The church of Jesus Christ has the power to resist the enemy and to bring

Jesus' rule to the Earth which will bring liberty to all. Jesus' plan is that through the church the manifold wisdom of God will be made known, just as it says in Ephesians 3:10, "**His intent** was that now, **through the church**, the manifold wisdom of God should be made known to the rulers and authorities in the heavenly realms."

It breaks my heart when I see believers living in spiritual poverty and desolation. When the church acts powerless and anemic, it hurts me. Jesus asked us to heal the sick, raise the dead, cleanse the lepers, drive out demons and tell people that the Kingdom of God is at hand. For many believers that seems like a dream (or even a nightmare) that is very far away from where they live. They are still struggling with the idea that they are forgiven. They're still fighting sin even though Jesus already dealt with it for them. They are still trying to qualify themselves even though Jesus has fully qualified them. They're still struggling to understand they are have authority and that they are seated in heavenly places in Christ. The worries of this world have strangled the life of God out of them.

The passion and purpose of this book is to re-ignite the life of God in you, for you to be connected with the fountain of life within. God the Father, the Son, and the Holy Spirit have taken up residence in you so that you can reflect His glory. You are God's beloved. He has loved you with an everlasting love. He has gone to enormous lengths to see you fully restored, healed, and empowered to live the life that He originally intended.

At some point, we as believers have to get over ourselves. At some point we have to believe that He loves us and that He is good. At some point we have to come to believe that we are forgiven and that we're done with sin. At some point we have to start to believe in who He says He is and who He says we are.

Let me ask you this question. If the church was not busy fighting sin (since Jesus already won that fight), was not busy fighting the devil (because Christ already did that and made a public spectacle of him), and was not busy fighting the world (judging the world as opposed to being useful and kind), then what would the church be doing? Think about it for a minute. This is a very serious question. The enemy has successfully focused us on things that Jesus has already accomplished for us on the cross. At some point the church needs to take her attention off fighting sin, the devil, and the world. If the church was not doing these things, she would be about the Father's business. Does that sound familiar? Jesus was about the Father's business and that business was an extraordinarily creative and wonderfully broad place. It is not a narrow-minded, lifeless, robotic existence which worldly thinking would lead us to believe. It is the most fulfilling, meaningful, and exciting existence that any human being on the planet could enjoy.

We've discovered God's truth and then gone on to find out that it's even better than we ever imagined. The Lord is so kind! He is so beautiful and wonderful! We find that every command that He's given us to do, He has also empowered us with divine power to do it.

We have been empowered and wired by God to be able to supernaturally function in His realm. We are able to put the forces of darkness on notice and put them to flight. We are able to see our communities restored by the power of Heaven. We have been given divine authority to rule our own spirit and to see the Kingdom of God manifest in every area of our own lives.

I hope that you're enormously encouraged by the idea that you have been given the supernatural capability to receive from God, relate to him, and respond in a way that releases all of Heaven in your life and in those around you.

Like Paul said, none of us have attained this by any means. We are all on a journey towards walking in all that Jesus intended for us. The purpose of this book is to create a framework to show that you have been wired to receive grace and to walk with the Holy Spirit in power. This is the calling and right of every believer on the planet.

Perhaps you are one of those blessed believers who attend the church that releases the life of God by helping people be transformed by experiencing grace and the Holy Spirit. If you are not, pray and ask the Holy Spirit to find you a spiritual home that will help you step into your full inheritance in Christ. Do not waste another day on theology of powerlessness designed to support intellectualized Christianity. Release yourself of the yoke of the law. Galatians 1 commands us to stand firm in our freedom and not to put ourselves again under the yoke of the law. If the preaching you're receiving is a mixture of law and grace, it may be time to find a different spiritual home. I say this not to put any church in judgment, but to bring freedom and liberty to believers who seek to walk in the fullness of all that God has for them.

It is time for you to enjoy the fountain of life within you, overflowing your spirit and saturating your heart. And out of the fullness of your heart, to saturate your sense of who you are - your soul. It is time to walk in abundant life. This pleases the Lord!

27

CHAPTER TWENTY SEVEN

PRACTICAL NEXT STEPS

This last chapter is focused on some practical steps to help you walk in the truth we've discussed in this book. To do this, I want to provide you with some daily confessions that you can read out loud. I recommend that you read one confession every day for 30 days. Each month use the next confession. The first 4 confessions will give you 120 days of mind-renewing confessions. Here is what they cover:

- Confession #1: Grace
- Confession #2: Your supernatural capacity to receive
- Confession #3: Your supernatural capacity to relate
- Confession #4: Your supernatural capacity to respond.

In addition to these confessions we will also talk about some **practical new nature habits** to help the life of God flow through you.

It is really important, as you grow up in the Lord and come to spiritual maturity in Christ, that you say the same things that God says about you. These confessions are confessing Christ and His finished work in your life. I recommend that you read them aloud every day. You will be amazed at how your mind will be transformed as you hear yourself read these words.

Confession #1

"I am a son/daughter of the Lord. The day I accepted Christ I became a new creation. Old things have passed away and all things have become new. Jesus has completely forgiven me of all my sins: past, present, and future. I am always forgiven and the Father has taken an oath not to hold my sin against me. I am free from sin. I am free from the law. I am free from worldliness. Jesus has completely cleansed my conscience and my past no longer has the power to define me. Only Jesus can define me. I have been given a new nature which loves to worship God and serve Him. I am seated with Christ in heavenly places. I have a brand-new standing with God the Father. I am now fully positioned to enjoy all the benefits there was due to Jesus. Everything that was on my account has been moved to Jesus' account. Everything there was due to Jesus' account has been moved to my account. I have been blessed with every spiritual blessing in heavenly places. I now enjoy the favor of the Lord and walk in His blessing. I am now fully qualified to enjoy my full inheritance in Christ because Jesus has fully qualified me. I enjoy the love of the Father and the fellowship of the Holy Spirit. From today on, I will walk in step with the Spirit so that I may access all that Jesus purchased for me at the cross and my life will please the Father."

Once you have used confession #1 one for 30 days, I recommend that you move to the next confession for the next 30 days.

Confession #2

"The Lord has given me supernatural capabilities in my human spirit so that I can live in His realm. I have been given the power from Heaven to receive abundant grace. The Holy Spirit leads me into all truth and I am able to receive revelation that supersedes my mental capacity to understand. I will receive revelation in my spirit and I will trust God to add understanding to my mind over time. With this capability, I'm able to understand the truth and not be deceived. I am able to receive God's purpose for my life and understand what He has called me to. Today, I will take the next step in walking in that purpose. Everything to do with my past has been forgiven and today I will receive healing for my body, healing for my emotions, and renewal for my mind. God has not given me a spirit of fear and of timidity, but of power and of a sound mind. I trust the Holy Spirit who searches the deep things of God to reveal to me all that He has for me. I choose from this day forward to live a life of power. Powerlessness is no longer acceptable to me. I invite you, Holy Spirit to well up inside my spirit and overflow into every aspect of my inner being. I invite you, Lord, to redefine me according to how Heaven knows me. I put aside worldly thinking and I accept the thoughts of Christ. Today I will allow those deep thoughts of God to flow through my spirit and into my mind. I will take captive every thought that is negative and destructive and bring it into submission to the truth of God's word. The mental strongholds that the enemy and the world has built in my mind, I now demolish in the name of Jesus. I bring all my problems to Jesus and cast all my burdens on Him because I know He cares for me. I trust fully that my problems are now in His hands and thereby free my mind to think positive thoughts. I will live a worry-free life by the power of Heaven. If today I discover that I've taken some of these problems back and find my mind worrying about them, I will immediately give them back to the Lord in prayer. I will continually put my problems in His hands until they stay there. I received the peace of the Lord in my life to guard my heart and mind. I choose to **let** the peace of Christ reign in me. I release the joy of the Lord to be my strength in the name of Jesus."

Confession #3

"I have been given authority to be a son/daughter of the Father. Today I will walk confidently knowing of His deep love for me. My mind is open to receive good gifts from Him because I know that all good gifts come from my Father above. I am not expecting God to talk to me about my old nature because my old nature is dead. I expect Him to speak to me about my new nature and about who I am in Him and His the promises for my future. I rejoice that Jesus is my heavenly Bridegroom and I am His beloved. Oh how He loves me! The Holy Spirit is my closest friend and I open my spirit to enjoy and receive His word. I have been given the supernatural ability to connect with truth and make it mine. Therefore, I will believe what God's word says about me. No longer will I see truth as an abstract concept reserved for the spiritually mature. I have a deep personal relationship with Truth Himself - Jesus. Every aspect of what Jesus has purchased for me I will make my own by the power of Heaven. I hereby authorize the peace of Christ to reign in me. I will **let** the message of Christ dwell in me richly. I will **let** perseverance have its full work in me so that I can grow up to maturity in Christ lacking nothing. Today I will ask the Holy Spirit to show me the upgrades that He has for me. I look at my trials and challenges of today with great joy because I know that they are mere wrappers for the upgrades God for me. I will not look at my circumstances through worldly eyes, but I will see them as a gift from the Lord to upgrade me and bring me to completeness in Him. Today, I will walk with awareness of the presence of the Lord. I know that I'm constantly in His presence and that nothing can separate me from His love. Today, I want to increase my awareness of what God is doing in my life and enjoy His tangible presence throughout my day."

Confession #4

"The Lord has endowed me with the supernatural ability to respond to Him in a way that pleases Him. God has given me capabilities in my spirit so that I can engage His world. I can bring the atmosphere of Heaven into my inner world and allow it to overflow to those around me. Today, I choose to be a worshipper and worship the Lord in spirit and in truth. Regardless of my mental state and my feelings, I will supersede the lesser functions of my heart (my mind, will, emotions, and conscience) and worship the Lord. I will bring glory to His name and bless Him. I choose today to rise up above my own personality and to worship and praise the Lord in complete liberty and freedom. I will shout for joy! I will rejoice in the Lord regardless of my circumstances and challenges. I know that He is faithful and that He can never not be faithful to me. I know that He loves me deeply. Today, I will use my supernatural authority to resist worldliness in my life. My narrative will be aligned with that of Heaven and will be positive. I will not allow my mouth to reflect the narrative of the world or the Kingdom of darkness. I will speak life to those around me and I will resist negativity and destruction. I declare war on my own negativity so that the life of God can overflow in me and through me. With God's authority I choose to see my life fully restored. All the years the locusts have eaten in my life, I claim back today in the name of Jesus. I know that God is a great Redeemer. He will redeem back the time I have wasted and lost. He will bring me into a new place of liberty and power. I submit myself to the work of the Holy Spirit in me to see all that God has for me, fully redeemed and restored back to me. Today I'll be sensitive to the Holy Spirit and look for opportunities to bless and restore others. Today, I will host the presence of Heaven and change the atmosphere of every situation I find myself in. In my home, my church, my family, my business, and my daily chores, I will host the atmosphere of Heaven. I will walk in peace. I will actively look to the Holy Spirit to bring words of encouragement and liberty to others today. Today, I will be about the Father's business and enjoy His company."

Walking in step with the Spirit

In addition to these confessions, I want to suggest **three new nature habits**. Before we discuss these habits, we need to take a moment to understand how habits work. Part of the process of our renewing our minds is putting new habits in place. I love what Graham Cooke says when he states that, "You do not have a sin nature, you have a sin habit."

We need to learn new habits to help function in the new life that Jesus has provided for us. When Jesus gave you the gift of righteousness, He expected you to develop the habit of walking in that righteousness. We discussed in the previous chapter that we are to train ourselves in godliness. One of the key ways to do that is to understand how to build godly habits.

How to build new nature habits

Let's look at the basic construction of how habits are formed. This diagram shows that all habits begin with a *Cue*:

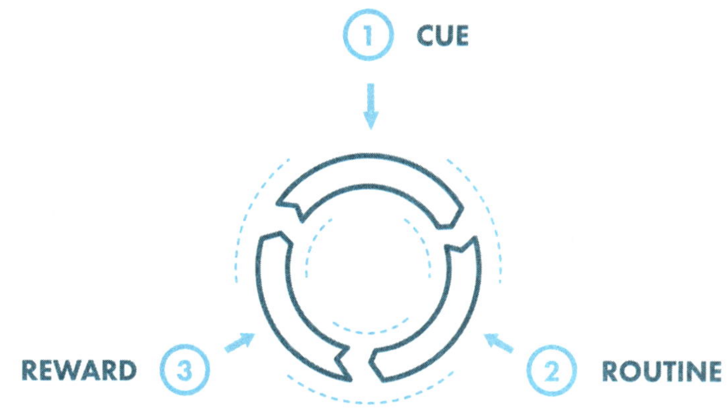

Did you know that 40% of what people do every day is not based on decisions but on habits? I recommend reading *The Power of Habit, Why we do what we do and how to change* By Charles Duhigg.

You know that you have been given supernatural power to change. You will discover that God has wired your brain to learn certain behaviors and store them as **automatic routines**.

Think about it like this: when you get in your car and drive to a shopping mall, you do not think about every little thing you are doing. Your brain has stored the techniques and behaviors of driving as an *automatic routine*. When you picked up your car keys you ignited a Cue.

This triggered your brain to call up the *driving routine* which then ran automatically requiring very little effort on your part. You were *rewarded* when you arrived at the shopping mall. This encourages you to trigger the Cue again.

But it was quite a different thing when you first learned to drive, wasn't it? The reason is that you had not yet developed the automatic *routines* in your brain. At first you picked up the key and you felt nervousness. You used the key to unlock the door. You got into the car and placed the key in the ignition. You turned the ignition until you found the key position that started the car. You had to put your foot on the brake while putting the car in reverse. You very carefully released your foot off the brake while you slowly reversed down the driveway. You looked in your mirror and held tightly onto the steering wheel. You were aware of every little step you were doing. When you finally turned into the street and applied the brake, you put the car in drive and began moving forward. Every traffic light and interaction with other drivers was a stressful and very focused process. It took enormous effort to make sure you did everything right and not drive into the curb or bump into another car.

After a while, these actions were programmed into your brain as *automatic routines*. Your brain became more and more efficient storing these routines in such a way that it used less thinking and energy. The day came when you could trigger those routines by simply picking up your car keys.

The same is true for spiritual habits. At first they take a lot of effort and feel unnatural. As you do them repetitively, they become part of your habit *routines*. You can build a library of these new nature habits. I am suggesting that every day you pick a time of the day when you wish to read your confessions. Next pick a specific *Cue* that will trigger your confession *routine*. As an example, when you sit down to read your

Bible (*Cue*) begin by reading your confession out loud. As you begin to do this, you develop the automatic *routine* in your mind. After a time, you will sit down to read your Bible and immediately be looking for your confession to read. When you read a confession out loud, and life is released into your inner being, you'll receive a great reward of truth, peace and joy. This will help reinforce the need to have that experience again. You will find yourself going through a cycle like this:

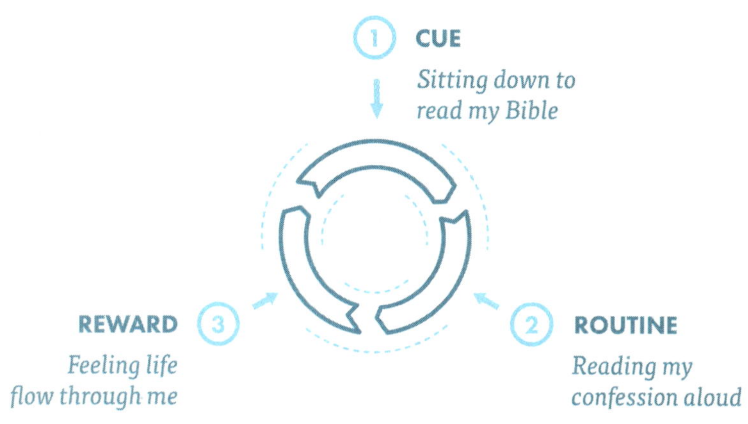

Of course, you can choose any Cue. It is best to make it something tangible.

Jogging as an example

Placing your running shoes next to your bed the night before will act as a Cue when you get up in the morning and see your running shoes. The running shoes act as a Cue to trigger the *Routine* of your morning jog. At first, going for this jog will feel somewhat stressful - like learning to drive. After a time, the entire process will be an automatic *routine* and take very little of your mental energy. You will get up in the morning, put on your running shoes, and will be back from your morning run before you've really thought about it.

You will have feelings of happiness, and even euphoria, just from the exercise experience itself. Mood-enhancing hormones and neurotransmitters including endorphins, endocannabinoids, dopamine and serotonin are released providing you with a strong *Reward*. This makes you want to have those feelings again, and you look forward to the next *Cue* so that you can be rewarded once more. You find yourself craving the *Rewards*. These are natural and healthy cravings. Spiritual rewards can also generate such spiritual cravings. These cravings please the Lord.

We can summarize the habit loop as follows:

- **Cue**: this is the trigger that causes the brain to go into automatic mode.
- **Routine**: this is an automatic routine that the brain stores because it has done it so many times before that it does not need to think about it.
- **Reward**: this is the physical, emotional, or spiritual reward we receive which reinforces our desire to have another trigger (Cue).

This is great news for you! As you develop new nature habits, you can make many spiritual habits automatic and effortless. How kind is the Lord to wire us in this way? It is truly wonderful that He has provided us with such remarkable capabilities. Think of what you can achieve as a new lifestyle if you combine the supernatural functions of your human spirit with this remarkable habit mechanism. Perhaps you now see how God has wired you for a lifestyle of abundant life. Studies show that when people **believe** they are able to change, change is far more likely. You have been given the supernatural functions to enable you to believe that you can walk in your new nature already given to you in Christ. **Jesus is the change agent**. You simply form the habit to walk in those changes. You are a new creation being with a new nature. Jesus did that for you.

Ask the Holy Spirit which habits He wants you to develop first. He is so excited about these possibilities for you and will be quick to show you which habits He wishes you to develop first. Please do not try to develop too many new habits at once. Allow the Lord to develop them in you since it takes 30 to 60 days for the brain to go into automatic mode.

Three new nature habits

I wish to encourage you to develop three new key habits. These habits will help you walk in your new nature and keep in step with the Spirit. They will help you walk in all the truth we have discussed in this book.

The drinking habit

We discussed the idea of learning to set time aside to receive from the Lord and exercise your supernatural capability to receive. In the same way that a thirsty person would drink cool clear water, a spiritual person drinks of the Lord and receives from Him. Remember Jesus said, "Let anyone who is thirsty come to me and drink. Whoever believes in me, as Scripture has said, rivers of living water will flow from within them." Spend five minutes every day simply receiving and drinking. This is not the time to pray or to praise. This is the time to open your spirit to the Holy Spirit and allow life to fill up on the inside and overflow from your spirit into your heart. This is why the Bible tells us to be continually filled with the Holy Spirit.

Here is a summary of this habit:

- **Cue**: the sense of feeling spiritually dry or depleted.
- **Routine**: spend five minutes drinking deeply of the Holy Spirit.
- **Reward**: the life of God overflowing your spirit into your heart.

The journaling habit

It is good stewardship, and certainly a great new nature habit, to write down what you believe the Holy Spirit is saying. Take a few minutes every day and do that. At the end of each month, take an additional 15 minutes to review everything God has said to you and you will be shocked and amazed at the clarity of His voice. His communication will be clear and consistent.

Here is a summary of this habit:

- **Cue**: {suggestion} after reading your Bible. (Choose any cue you like)
- **Routine**: write down what you believe the Holy Spirit is saying to you
- **Reward**: clarity of what God is doing in and for you.

The free mind habit

This is one of the most powerful habits I can share with you. This new nature habit will empower you to live a worry-free life. Remember the three-step process to free your mind. Step 1: take captive any negative thought. Step 2: pray and deal with all negative thoughts and problems in prayer. Step 3: free your mind to focus on positive things - whatsoever things are True, Admirable and Pure (TAP).

- **Cue**: worry or anxiety.
- **Routine**: take the negative thought captive. Pray and give it to the Lord immediately. Think TAP thoughts.
- **Reward**: a free and creative mind enjoying an anxiety-free life.

The Supernatural becoming natural

It is natural for God to think the way He does. You are in Him so so it will become natural to think like He does. There will come a time that it no longer seems to be supernatural but natural to you. You were born to live like this and to think like God thinks. Your ways will become like His ways. **This is your new natural.**

We have come to the end of our journey together. I hope that you are enormously encouraged now that you realize how God has wired you. As you enjoy your freedom in the gospel of grace and walking in step with the Holy Spirit, I pray that you will come to maturity in Christ and enjoy your glorious inheritance. I pray that God would use you richly to transform those around you and the community in which you live. I pray for the richness of His fellowship and a continual sense of His presence to become a true reality in your life. As you walk in your freedom from sin, the law, and the world, enjoy the richness of the abundant life Jesus purchased for you!